Managing Dyadic Interactions in Organizational Leadership

Managing Dyadic Interactions in Organizational Leadership

Kanika T. Bhal
Mahfooz A. Ansari

Sage Publications
New Delhi ◄ Thousand Oaks ► London

First published in 2000 by

Sage Publications India Pvt Ltd
M-32 Market, Greater Kailash, Part 1
New Delhi 110 048

Sage Publications Inc.
2455 Teller Road
Thousand Oaks, California 91320

Sage Publications Ltd
6 Bonhill Street
London EC2A 4PU

Published by Tejeshwar Singh for Sage Publications India Pvt Ltd, typeset by Line Arts, Pondicherry and printed at Chaman Enterprises, Delhi.

Library of Congress Cataloging-in-Publication Data

Bhal, Kanika T., 1964–
  Managing dyadic interactions in organizational leadership/Kanika T. Bhal, M.A. Ansari.
    p. cm.
  Includes bibliographical references and index.
  1. Leadership 2. Communication in management. I. Ansari, Mahfooz A., 1949– II. Title.

HD57.7.B49   658.4'092—dc21   2000   00–055390

ISBN: 0–7619–9483–1 (US-HB)   81–7036–960–6 (India-HB)

Typeset in 10/12 Charter BT.

Sage Production Team: Jaya Chowdhury, Radha Dev Raj and Santosh Rawat

Contents

List of Tables

Preface

Much has been written on organizational leadership but the concept still remains elusive. This present volume focuses on a hitherto relatively less explored dimension of leadership, viz., the quality of interaction in leader–member dyads, shifting the focus from only leaders to both leaders and followers. The underlying tenet is the fact that different subordinates have different relationships with the leader and it is this variation that is the focus of our inquiry. This explains the process of leadership by treating the subordinates as active participants in the leadership process. These tenets are tested through rigorous scientific research and empirical data.

The present volume is divided into six chapters. The first chapter contains an introduction to the foundations of our above-mentioned approach which ends with a proposed model for the present investigations. Chapter 2 contains the methodological details. The first part of the chapter contains details of our first work (Study 1)—research site, participants, and the measures used. The second part contains the same details of our corroborative study (Study 2). The next three chapters deal with the results of these studies and their implications. In Chapter 3, the details of scale development are given. After presenting a review of the previous scales in the first part of the chapter, the statistical properties of the newly developed scale are given in the second part. In the last part of the chapter, the level of the scale is established. The antecedent conditions are discussed in Chapter 4. Three major antecedent interactions are discussed in the three parts of this chapter. Part one contains the interaction of the personal attributes of the leader and the member—the background, hypotheses, and results and discussion. Parts two and three contain the same details of the interaction of leadership orientations and the interaction of personal attributes with climate, respectively. The third objective of evaluating outcomes is discussed in Chapter 5. The first part contains the use of influence strategies to influence each other (leader and member) as outcomes of their quality of interaction. Part two contains other outcomes, like satisfaction, commitment, etc. of the members. Finally, the results are summarized and overall implications are given in Chapter 6. The Indian social milieu and the Indian value system are given due importance while suggesting the implications of the two survey findings.

A volume like this is an outcome of the efforts of many people—scholars, students, managers, and positive thinkers. Some contribute tangibly others not so tangibly. Professor Graen and Professor Fred Dansereau's initiatives in the field were the inspirations to take up the project; we thank them for their inspiring work. My good friend Dr Uma Lakhtakia, at the University of Mauritius, generously spared her time. Dr Sangeeta Dhawan, now at the Indian Institute of Management, Lucknow, also provided support at crucial times of this research.

We are indebted to our academic colleagues who contributed to this volume at different stages. Professor S.A. Shaida and Professor B.N. Patnaik provided the support for and insight into the research. I also thank all my friends: J.J., Nagarjuna, Vandana, Seema, and Sanil for doing their best in more ways than one. Their thoughtfulness and understanding are deeply felt and warmly appreciated. Vijay's assistance and meticulous typing too are sincerely appreciated.

We are thankful to the top executives of organizations for helping in data collection and to the respondents for sharing their world-views. Without their help, this work would not have been possible.

Anand's encouragement and support remain a constant source of inspiration. Finally, thanks are due to my son Yash, but for whose love and affection I would have completed this book two months earlier.

Kanika T. Bhal
New Delhi
August, 2000

◀ Chapter 1 ▶

The Foundations of the Dyadic Approach

The relevance and centrality of leadership in organizations cannot be overemphasized in light of the fact that in most cases the failure of the new organizations right at the start is because of poor leadership (Schultz, 1982). The faith of the organizations in effective and efficient leadership is reflected in the amount of effort, energy, and above all money that the organizations spend in hiring and maintaining their leaders. Because of its importance, the phenomenon has been most widely read, however, it remains least understood. Because of the dynamic and multifaceted nature of the construct, focusing on any one aspect never gives the overall picture and yields abortive results. Most of the researches, theories, and understandings of the phenomenon have focused only on the leader him- or herself but have ignored an equally important component—the 'led' or the subordinate. Most of the traditional theories treat the group of subordinates as a homogeneous entity that is a passive recipient of all leadership efforts. Subsequently, the group as a unit is taken to respond collectively to leadership attempts. These theorizations wittingly or unwittingly totally overlook the kind of interactions that may develop between a leader and an individual subordinate, thereby making an average assumption about the work-group. The present work not only incorporates the subordinate but also explores the interaction between a leader and a member in understanding the phenomenon of leadership. We begin by pointing out the average nature of all the earlier theorizations, then explore the nature of dyadic leadership.

Leadership: The Average Approach

The earliest understandings of leadership focused on traits or fixed personality characteristics as determinants of effective leadership. However, despite a host of studies, the researches could not converge on a set of traits that could predict effective leadership (Byrd, 1940; Stogdill, 1948). Clearly, trait theories make average assumptions about the work-group.

The next set of theorists focused on the acts or behaviors of the leader and the focus was on identifying 'what leaders do' as opposed to the trait-oriented focus on 'what leaders have.'

A series of studies were initiated in 1945 by the Bureau of Business Research under the headship of C.L. Shartle. The first objective of this effort was, of course, to unearth the various leader behaviors. In the first phase of the research, a questionnaire was to be developed. Beginning with 1,800 examples of leader behavior, the identification boiled down to 150 items that were contained in the Leader Behavior Description Questionnaire (LBDQ). The responses to these items were factor analyzed and the analysis showed that the subordinates perceived their leader's behavior in terms of two distinct categories (Fleishman, 1953, 1957; Halpin & Winer, 1957; Hemphill & Coons, 1957). Subsequently, these two behavior categories were called 'Consideration' and 'Initiating Structure.' They were characterized as follows:

> Consideration included behavior items concerned with leader supportiveness, friendliness, consideration, consultation with subordinates, representation of subordinate interests, openness of communication with subordinates and recognition of subordinate contributions.

> Initiating Structure included behavior items concerned with directing subordinates, clarifying subordinate roles, planning, coordinating, problem solving, criticizing poor work and pressurizing subordinates to perform better (Yukl, 1981, p. 106).

Thus, consideration parallels a 'relationship' aspect and initiating structure the 'work' aspect. All the behavioral approaches ultimately identified the same two dimensions, viz., focus on people and focus on task (Blake & Mouton, 1964; Katz, Maccoby & Morse, 1950). Though behavioral approach studied a more malleable aspect of leader behavior, it prescribed a combination of high people and high task orientation for effective leadership, again leaving no scope for variability within a work-group of subordinates.

Lack of support for one effective or ideal leadership style led to the inclusion of situational variables in the leadership equation. A component of situational variability was identified which was expected to contribute to the effectiveness of one leadership style over the other. Consequently, a host of situations were identified as contributing to leadership effectiveness that included aspects of favorability–unfavorability (Fiedler, 1967) and the maturity of the subordinates (Hersey & Blanchard, 1982). In the Indian context J.B.P. Sinha (1980) identified the meta values as a situational contingency relevant to delineate effective leader behavior. It needs to be mentioned here that though all the contingency theories treat the subordinates as a homogeneous entity, Hersey and Blanchard, and Sinha recognize the possibility of variation across subordinates. However, there are two points of relevance here. First, these theories are prescriptive and advise the leader to vary his or her style depending upon the maturity level of the subordinates. Second, and consequently, there is absolutely no notion of the subordinate being an active partner in the exchange process. In a sense then they too treat subordinates as passive entities. Situational contingency theories too do not incorporate the dynamic inputs of the subordinates.

Any reference to leadership research would be incomplete without incorporating the newer developments. The turbulence of the modern day business environment and the need to constantly change and provide vision has directed leadership research towards the transformational nature of organizational leadership. J.M. Burns (1978) studied the two types of leaders, viz., the transactional and transformational in political context, wherein he identified transactional leaders as those who deal with their followers on the basis of exchange—jobs for votes or subsidies for campaign. However, the transformational leaders go further and recognize higher needs of the people and engage the full person instead of interacting through exchanges. Transformational leadership hence has been associated with charisma and other traits related to leaders.

Leadership theorization seems to have come full circle by identifying traits like selflessness, will power to persist, courage to decide, and self-insight for leadership effectiveness (Chibber, 1995). These theorizations, obviously, have no scope for identifying the subordinate-related variables in their understanding of leadership.

Leadership: The Alternative VDL Approach

As a reaction to the averaging tendency of all the major formulations, an alternative Vertical Dyadic Linkage (VDL) theory has been developed. The theory is a comprehensive one. It begins to investigate the actual phenomenon of leadership as it occurs at a dyadic level in organizations and then tries to understand the phenomenon in terms of other organizational events or phenomena. It does not prescribe leadership behavior or style; it only attempts to investigate the process as it actually occurs in organizations by identifying the unique fact that leaders differentiate between the members of a group. In the organizational setting where leaders do not emerge, but are appointed, an understanding of the work-unit functioning is a must to understand leadership. It will be pointed out in the next section (on theoretical bases), how it may become important for the leader to have a differential relationship with the members because of external demands. The model, by taking into account the leader's behavior, takes care of the elements, and by recognizing the phenomenon of unit differentiation also incorporates processes involved in leadership. Thus, the theory is a confluence of elements and processes involved in leadership.

Conceptualizations

An alternative understanding of the leadership phenomenon stems from the fact that the leader can and does behave differently with different subordinates in a work-group.

All the other leadership models (as mentioned earlier) are average because of the two assumptions they implicitly make. First, all the members in a unit are treated as a homogeneous lot, so far as their work experiences are concerned. Consequently, they are all clubbed together and are treated as one entity—the 'work-group.' Second, the leader is believed to behave essentially in the same (consistent) manner towards all the subordinates. This leads to averaging leader behavior over the work-group (Dansereau, Cashman, & Graen, 1973). However, these assumptions get falsified in the Average Leadership Style (ALS) framework itself. The leader's self ratings and the work-group ratings of the leader behavior show near zero correlations (Evans, 1970).

The VDL approach focuses on the leader–member dyad as the unit of analysis. In this perspective, then, the leader's interactions with individual subordinates are of prime importance. By focusing on the dyadic relationship, we do not rule out the possibility of average style. Instead, it provides a test for *both*. If the responses in all the dyads are similar, they can indeed be averaged.

The relative stand of the two approaches with respect to each other was evaluated in an earlier study by Dansereau et al. (1973). They concluded:

'...this VDL approach reveals orderliness in the data that the average leadership style would have assumed *a priori* to be mainly error variance. On the other hand, orderliness revealed by the VDL approach could not have been extracted from the data using the ALS approach' (ibid., p. 197).

The theory posits that the leaders do behave differently with different subordinates (Dansereau, Graen, & Haga, 1975). Although each dyad has a unique interaction or leader–member exchange (LMX), theoretically, two extreme interactions are of interest. The two extremes are the good and the poor quality of exchanges. They have been variously labeled: leadership and supervisory relationships (Dansereau et al., 1975), the informal assistants and the ordinary members (Graen, 1976), the IN/OUT-Group relationships (Graen & Cashman, 1975), or high and low quality relationships (Graen & Schiemann, 1978).

According to this theory, the members have different interactions with their leader because they define their roles differently—a result of different dynamics involved in the role development process by different members. Though the model recognizes the fact of unit differentiation it does not state that differentiation leads to effectiveness. In this sense, the model is not prescriptive; instead, it is a factual understanding of the leadership process.

The unit differentiation under a leader follows an exchange process between the leader and the individual member. As a part of which some members put in more efforts in terms of energy and time to collaborate with the leader. These members get favors of different kinds in return. Dansereau et al. (1975) portray IN-Group exchanges as being characterized by interactions over and above the organizational contract. On the other extreme, the interaction between a leader and a member is essentially contractual. The member puts in only that much of work as is given in the organizational contract. In return, they get only organizationally prescribed outcomes (Dansereau et al., 1975). This distinction in leader behavior has its roots in leadership and supervisory behaviors wherein leadership is influencing without recourse to formal authority (Jacobs, 1970).

Although Jacobs recognizes this variability in leader behavior, the members' perspective is not evaluated. It is, therefore, not clear whether the members perceive the difference in leadership techniques or not. The VDL theory incorporates both the subordinate and the leader perspectives.

If indeed the subordinates perceive the difference in leader behavior, their organizational experiences are bound to be different. Be it satisfaction, commitment, or performance; as long as the frame of reference is leadership, the focus of attention should be the individual members. As Dansereau et al. (1975, p. 72) discovered: '... the attitudes and reactions (turnover) of the members (in-group) clearly reflected the reward value of differential treatment over time.'

The integrated framework of the VDL model is now presented. The theoretical bases reveal how these unique relationships develop along with role development (by the members) through the process of social exchange.

Theoretical Bases

In the following sub-sections, an attempt is made to trace the roots of unit differentiation. If unit differentiation is so universally present, what are the reasons or explanations for the same.

The Background: Negotiability of Roles

The VDL theory explains the leadership phenomenon in a developmental perspective. The unique interaction that develops between a leader and a member is an outcome of role development by the members. How the members develop their roles through interpersonal exchanges with their leader forms the crux of the theory. To fit the leadership phenomenon in a broad organizational framework, let us begin with the understanding of organizations and the place of roles in this understanding.

A systemic approach views the organization as

> 'energic input-output systems ... Social organizations are flagrantly open systems in that the input of energies and the conversion of output into further energic input consists of transactions between the organization and its environment' (Katz & Kahn, 1978, p. 20).

Thus, an organization imports energy from the environment (input), works upon it (throughput), and exports the product to the environment (output). This process of energic exchange is cyclical and the survival of the organization depends upon the maintenance of these cycles. In other words, these cyclical processes constitute the structure (Allport, 1954, 1967) of an organization. What are the mechanisms and structures involved in these processes? These processes are the outcome of coordinated activities of the office-holders or occupants in the organization. These coordinated activities present an interwoven and cohesive network. It is this network then, that constitutes an organization. This discussion highlights two important aspects of the organization: (*i*) organizations owe their existence to the network of coordinated activities of people, and (*ii*) organizations are open systems and, hence, are in constant interaction with the environment.

To understand the social aspects of the organization, one focuses on the activities of components or office-holders. The organizational plan is made up of some nodal points. These nodal points have some particular functions to perform in the network. The nodal points are the offices, and the people occupying these offices are the occupants or office-holders. There are some relevant prescribed behaviors associated with each office. It is these prescribed behaviors or behavior patterns that constitute a *role*. Thus in the final analysis, an organization is a 'network of standardized behaviors' (Katz & Kahn, 1978, p. 45).

If the roles or behaviors of nodal occupants are fixed and static, the organizations should also be rigid and static. As mentioned before, organizations are in constant interaction with the environment. Therefore, any changes in the environment necessitate equivalent changes in the organization. Since the environment is dynamic and modern-day environment is marked with extreme transience (Dunnette, 1972), organizations must dynamically adapt to these changes for their survival (Bennis, 1966). The organizations will be dynamic and negotiable only when its constituents, i.e., the roles are dynamic and negotiable (Barnard, 1938).

At the grassroot level, these negotiations are the negotiations between the individual members (role occupants) and the organization. Thus, the process of negotiation involves inducements and contributions (Barnard, 1938) from both the parties—the organization and the role occupant. A dynamic conceptualization of organization would expect its members to put in more efforts to cope with the added new responsibilities. For this purpose, the organization offers rewards and resources that the role occupants might value, and seek their services in return. Schein (1980) calls this two-way influence relationship, the 'psychological contract.' Thus, negotiation takes place mostly for the unstructured, unforeseen tasks. So far, we have touched upon exchanges but only hypothetically. Organization can neither offer rewards nor can it seek services directly, we now delineate the appropriate level to study these exchanges.

Dyad: The Unit of Negotiation

The fact concerning the negotiations is well taken, but how is it that these negotiations take place? This question will be addressed a little later, for the moment, let us see at what level these exchanges take place.

Since the very notion of exchange involves a participation of at least two parties, the individual level is ruled out. To delineate the unit of analysis, let us go back to the systemic conceptualization of an organization. The interwoven network of activities forms the organizational structure. This interweaving will involve at least two people, to begin with. Organizing, in this sense, is viewed as the process of interlocking of the individual behavior between two or more people (Weick, 1979). A unit of this interlocking will involve an action by one role occupant and a reaction to it by another role occupant. This cycle of action by one and reaction by another is called a double interact (ibid.). Thus, at the most basic level, interaction occurs at the level of double interacts. These are the units that describe interpersonal influence (Hollander, 1976). In an organizational framework, one conceives of several inter-locked behavior cycles of these double interacts which are embed-ded in the larger system. As Weick (1979, p. 112) points out, 'it is these cycles that are the stable forms within organizations, and it is these cycles that are embedded into larger subassemblies in the interest of stabilizing equivocal displays and transforming them into information, enacted environments and cause maps.'

Thus, the right unit of analysis is a dyad. Next, we examine how and/or through what processes these exchanges take place.

Role Development and the Leader

The bureaucratic conceptualizations treated organizations as fixed entities. Hence they asked for a routine machine-like adherence to norms by the members. This precluded any development or negoti-ation in roles. But, as has been pointed out, roles are flexible and negotiable, there is a scope for the development of roles by individ-ual members. Kahn, Wolfe, Quinn, Snoek, and Rosenthal (1964) proposed a role episode model of role development by the organi-zational members. This was in response to the incompleteness of the fixed organizational design. To understand this, let us go back once again to the structure of an organization. Organization is a network of interdependent activities. An occupant takes up a posi-tion in this network. We call him or her the focal person. Some offices will be closer to this focal person than others. Since the activities are interdependent, all these positions or offices (that are closer) will be affected by the activities of the person at that partic-ular position. All such positions or offices that are directly affected by the role performance of the focal member constitute the *role-set* of the focal member (Merton, 1957). These are the people who try to influence the role performance of the focal member. How they do this has been understood in terms of *role-episode*. The different members of the role-set send information about the role to the focal member. The member receives the information and makes a response. The response is sent back to the role sender. Thus, a role-episode consists of a 'complete cycle of role sending, response by the focal person, and the effects of that response on the role send-ers' (Kahn et al., 1964, p. 26). Thus, besides the technological and authority-based demands, there are some interpersonal demands that are placed on the focal member by the role-set.

The most important role-set for the focal member is his or her immediate superior (Graen, 1976; Graen & Scandura, 1987), because it is the immediate superior only who has a formal and direct control over organizational resources (Katz & Kahn, 1978). If the leader is indeed the most important role-set, what will the leader's concern be when he or she sends information to the member through role-episodes?

Let us examine the areas where the leader needs the members' help (role performance) and defines leadership in that context. As stated a while ago, owing to a transience in the environment, organizations are constantly faced with new or unforeseen situations and tasks. As a result, leaders too are faced with these unforeseen, unstructured tasks. Working on these tasks is not a part of the formal organizational contract of the members. All the same, the leader has to get the task done from his or her subordinates and for this he or she has to use influence which is not a part of the organizational contract. In this light, hence, leadership is *'the influential increment over and above the mechanical compliance with the routine directives of the organization'* (Katz & Kahn, 1978, p. 528, emphases in original). Although Katz and Kahn have used the definition in the power bases framework, the definition fits the present conceptualization and hence is employed in the present research.

Negotiation and Unit Differentiation

An overall observation of the foregoing discussion seems to suggest that the phenomenon of leadership be studied with reference to unstructured tasks. Unstructured tasks are undefined, ambiguous contingencies. By their very nature, they allow for multiple task formulations. They are characterized by a number of goals to be attained and a number of ways (means) to attain these goals. They lack well-defined ends and means, as they arise from environmental changes. As a consequence, they cannot be reduced to standard organizational procedures. Nevertheless, some members do have to work for these jobs in order for the organization to survive.

If leaders too are faced with these unstructured tasks, then how is it that the leader works on them? The leader does need the collaboration of members on these jobs. Since all members are not obliged to work on these unstructured tasks, the leader develops an interaction only with a few members who collaborate with him or her.

How some members get to collaborate with the leader has been understood in terms of role development. The contention is that some members incorporate working on unstructured task as a part of their role. This is a result of the role development by these members with the leader as the role-set. Next, we take up the process of role development by the members.

Role Development by the Members

The process of role development by the members, with the leader as a role-set, has been aptly delineated by Graen and Scandura (1987). The following discussion draws heavily upon their thesis. The process is understood with the backdrop of unstructured tasks, as roles become negotiable only for such tasks. Structured tasks demand a prescribed role adherence from the members. Thus, in the whole process of role development the leader and the member get coordinated. The three stages are—role taking, role making, and role routinization (Figure 1.1).

Role Taking

This is the initial phase wherein the leader evaluates the relevant skills of the members. At this stage, the behaviors of both the parties are stereotypical (Altman & Taylor, 1973) and formal. The leader evaluates the members' motivation, orientations, skills, etc. through repeated role-episodes. A typical role-episode at this stage includes evaluation by the leader.

The leader puts across his or her expectations in the form of a role to the member. The member receives it and matches it with his or her own orientations, skills, etc. Based on this the member makes an appropriate response. The leader perceives the response against his or her own expectations. Following this the leader decides whether to evaluate the member further, go on to the next stage, or give up further negotiation. If the member does not come up to the leader's expectations, no further negotiations take place and the exchanges between them remain contractual. The evaluation is usually done through repeated role-episodes. As the background is contractual, the leader evaluates the members through structured tasks that are a part of the organizational givens. The member gets socialized into the formal organizational structure.

The leader is the active initiator at this stage. 'Clearly, the superior acts and the member reacts; the superior is an active problem solver and the member is a passive responder' (Graen & Scandura, 1987, p. 181). Leader expectations of subordinates established and expressed during the first few days of working together have been shown to be related to subordinate perceptions of the quality of leader–member exchanges six months later (Liden, Wayne, & Stilwell, 1993). In the next stage of role making, actual exchanges between the leader and the member take place.

Role Making

Active social exchange is the hallmark of this stage. Once the initial stage is over, the dyadic relationship starts taking a shape. The leader offers the member an opportunity to work on different tasks. He or she makes the offer and the member makes a response. The leader presents an opportunity to the member to work on unstructured tasks. The offer contains the leader's expectation about the member's input (working relationship) and the rewards that the member gets in return. The member evaluates the offer in terms of his or her own capabilities and attractiveness of the reward. On the basis of this, the member sends his or her own expectations and inputs. The leader finally evaluates the member's response against the initial offer and acts accordingly.

Social exchange theory provides the dominant theoretical basis for LMX (Sparrowe & Liden, 1997). Since the interaction is based on exchanges, a perception of 'equity' or 'fairness' by both the parties is a must for the exchanges to continue or grow (Homans, 1961). Additionally, each party must have resources that are valuable to the other. The member on his or her part should have the relevant skills, know-how, and motivation, and the leader must have resources to offer to the member. Over repeated exchanges of this kind, a working relationship develops between the two wherein both the parties have a knowledge of appropriate transactions. In the final phase, this coupling of behavior gets routinized.

Role Routinization

In this phase, the coupling gets crystallized. There are no overt exchanges between the leader and the member. The member works on unstructured tasks with the leader, as it becomes a part of the member's role. The two are totally interdependent for relevant tasks. A kind of dyadic understanding develops between the two. If one took a cross section of the dyad at this phase, it will be characterized with positive relational dimensions, the details of which are taken up in Chapter 3.

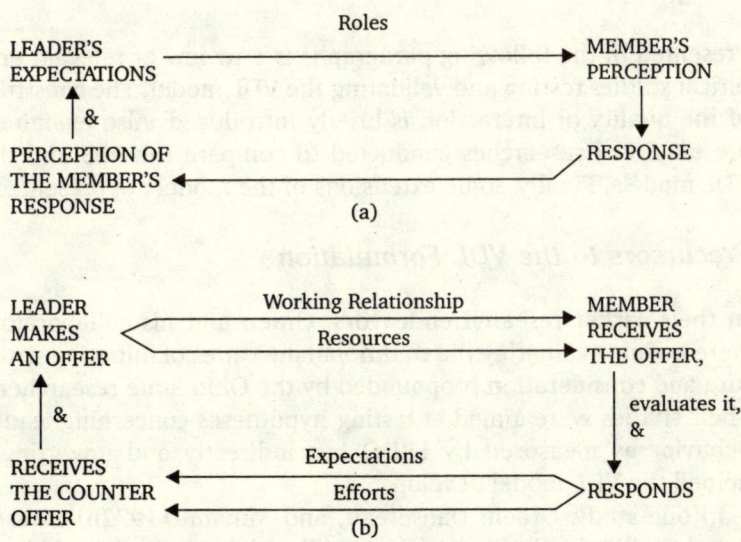

Figure 1.1: **Role Development by Members: (a) Typical Role Taking and (b) Typical Role Making Episodes.**

The Continuous Nature of Exchanges

The foregoing discussion shows the development of a differential unit. A too simplistic view of this would mean that the work-group under a leader gets differentiated into two sets of members—those who collaborate with the leader on unstructured tasks (IN-Group) and those who do not (OUT-Group). The exchanges are taken to be continuous, so that they can be placed on a continuum.

Two discrete categories would be acceptable if one divides the jobs into two categories—structured and unstructured. But structure is not all-or-none quantity. The structure or unstructure in a task can vary on a continuum. Naturally, the quality or quantity of exchanges too would vary on a continuum. This gives rise to a unit which is differentiated on a continuous basis.

The theoretical bases presented above clearly show as to how the unit differentiation takes place and how it is imperative in organizations. Now, let us look at some studies conducted to substantiate the theory.

An Update

Presented in the following paragraphs is a review of relevant empirical studies testing and validating the VDL model. The construct of the quality of interaction is briefly introduced. Also examined are empirical researches conducted to compare the ALS and the VDL models. Finally, some extensions of the model are presented.

Precursors to the VDL Formulation

In their earlier research endeavors, Graen and his collaborators were mainly evaluating the traditional measures of initiating structure and consideration propounded by the Ohio State researchers. Their studies were aimed at testing hypotheses concerning leader behavior as measured by LBDQ but indirectly and unwittingly helped the VDL model develop.

In one study, Graen, Dansereau, and Minami (1972b) investigated conflict for the man-in-the-middle. The man-in-the-middle is a manager trapped between his or her subordinates and his or her leader. These managers were analyzed in terms of two leader behavior dimensions. Their analysis indicated that, at lower organizational levels, both the superiors and the subordinates evaluated the man-in-the-middle favorably, if he or she initiated more structure.

In another study, they (Graen, Dansereau, & Minami, 1972a) evaluated the statistical interaction of initiating structure with consideration, and found that the correlation between the subordinate performance and leader consideration was positive for very high or low structure. On the other hand, for moderate structuring, the same correlation was near zero.

In yet another study, they aimed at testing the relative predictive power of expectancy and equity theories (Dansereau et al., 1973). The findings of these studies do not have any direct bearing on the model, nor were they aimed to do so. Yet, they are important because they employed individual level of analysis as opposed to the averages used in traditional studies. Hence, they are the much needed empirical base on which the VDL theory was developed later (Miner, 1980).

In the next set of studies, though the specific aim was not to test the dyadic assumptions, these studies and their findings fitted in the theoretical bases (role behavior) of the theory. Johnson and Graen (1973) conducted a study over a period of 16 weeks. They found that all those who left employment towards the end had experienced greater role conflict in earlier stages. Also, these people had an ambiguous relationship with their leader. In an extension of the same study, Graen, Orris, and Johnson (1973) found that those people who did not consider their jobs career relevant showed more turnover. More importantly, these people had less communication with their leaders and participated less in decision-making. The hypotheses were not aimed at testing within-group variance in terms of IN/OUT-Groups. At the same time, the standing of the subordinates in these studies corresponds to the OUT-Group.

In yet another study, Haga, Graen, and Dansereau (1974) found that more professionally oriented people indulged more in the role making or negotiation activities.

The designs of the forementioned studies were not to predict the outcomes for IN/OUT-Group subordinates. All the same, they lend heavy support to the fact that the subordinates' outcomes are a function of their relationships with the leader. These studies did lead to a formal conceptualization of the theory, as they focused on the individual's relationship with the leader.

Comparison of the ALS and the VDL Approaches

As has been made amply clear in the preceding sections, ALS models assume that 'the behaviour of the leader is in fact reasonably constant for all members' (Seeman, 1957, p. 95), thereby presuming the work-group to be homogeneous. Statistically, the unit of analysis in this case is the work-unit. In contrast, the proponents of the VDL theory claim that 'that appropriate level of analysis is not the work unit ... but the vertical dyad' (Graen & Cashman, 1975, p. 150). They (Dansereau et al., 1975; Graen, 1976; Graen & Cashman, 1975) argue that since the ALS approach presumes the leader behavior to be uniform across all members, the deviation within a unit is treated as error variance and is eventually ignored. They assert that it is this assumption of homogeneity that is responsible for 'such a slow progress in the leadership area' (Dansereau et al., 1975, p. 47). Hence, their focus is on variations within the group and they hold that the leader–member dyad is the appropriate unit of analysis. In view of these conflicting assertions, some reviews of leadership research emphasize the importance of studying and exploring the differences between these two approaches (e.g., Schriesheim & Kerr, 1977).

In line with this need, Schriesheim (1979) evaluated the relative validity of the two. For this purpose, subordinates' responses about their leaders' behavior were taken with two frames of reference—(*i*) leaders' behavior towards the individual subordinate, and (*ii*) the leaders' behavior towards the group as a whole. The results showed a very high correlation between the two. This implies that the members do not perceive any difference in their leader's behavior towards themselves individually as well as the work-group as a whole. The high correlation is probably because of the measure used. LBDQ XII has items which aim at the leader's group behavior—a reason behind the inflated results.

One way of comparing the two models is by evaluating individual responses in terms of the group responses. Statistically, the obtained variance is partitioned into within-group and between-group effects (WABA) (Dansereau & Dumas, 1977; Markham,

Dansereau, & Alutto, 1979). In other words, the responses of individuals can be broken down into two elements. One element is the between-group effects wherein the individual responses are averaged for a group giving one score for the group. These scores for different groups are compared. The other is the within-group effects wherein individual responses are compared with respect to the group means.

Katerberg and Hom (1981) conducted a study employing hierarchical multiple regression analysis to compare within-group and between-group variations. Based on their results, they conclude: 'the present results clearly indicate that within-group variation in leader behaviour continues to predict criteria even after the confounding effects of between-groups leadership variation are removed' (ibid., p. 220).

Vecchio (1982) replicated the above study in a field experimental setting. He reported that 'the results of the hierarchical regression analysis for the attitudinal measures successfully replicated Katerberg and Hom's findings' (ibid., p. 205). But neither the ALS nor the VDL approaches could predict the performance of the subordinates.

Graen, Liden, and Hoel (1982) compared the two approaches for predicting the outcome of turnover. They conclude: '... it is the unique exchange that develops between a leader and a member, not a leader's overall style, that influences a member's decision to remain in the organization' (ibid., p. 871).

This is a finding that was replicated for an all-female sample of nurses and their supervisors in another study (Ferris, 1985). All the same, Vecchio (1985) did not find similar results for subordinates at a lower organizational level in yet another replication of the Graen, Liden, and Hoel (1982) study.

Dansereau and colleagues were chiefly concerned with the development of the multiplexed approach to compare the levels of analysis. In the process, they analyzed the construct of 'negotiating latitude' from the Dansereau et al. (1975) study (Nachman, Dansereau, & Naughton, 1983). They used the WABA approach to compare the ALS and VDL approaches. The results showed systematic correlations for both between- and within-correlations. The objective was to test whether negotiating latitude was the dyadic phenomenon or the group phenomenon. It was also observed that there were individual differences which were neither at the dyadic level nor at the group level (Dansereau, Alutto, Markham, & Dumas, 1982). On the other hand, this result can also be interpreted at the dyadic level wherein the leader and the member interact on a 'one-to-one basis independently of either person's relationship with others outside of that dyad' (Nachman, Dansereau, & Naughton, 1985, p. 661).

Thus, the right question for enquiry is not which model is a better predictor: ALS or VDL. The need, now, is to examine the two as simultaneous processes.

Operationalizations of LMX

The construct to measure the exchanges between a leader and a member has been conceptualized in many different ways. The various operationalizations have received detailed treatment in Chapter 3. Different measuring instruments with different bases have been formulated. At this stage, it will be sufficient to say that the operationalization of the construct is sketchy. Thus, a psychometrically sound measure, which corresponds well with the basic theorizations of the VDL, needs to be developed.

Antecedents of LMX

The fact about the differentiated unit is well taken. True, the leader differentiates between the subordinates. But, what are the factors that determine the quality of exchanges between a leader and a member? These factors might come from the leader, the member, and/or the organizational structure. There have been a few attempts at identifying these variables (e.g., Bruning & Cashman, 1978). On the whole, the research is impoverished in this area.

Graen and Cashman (1975) suggested that 'the compatibility of some combination of members' characteristics and some combination of leaders' characteristics' (ibid., p. 155) could be an important determinant of the quality of exchange.

Although the compatibility hypothesis was not directly tested, Wakabayashi and Graen (1984) examined the effects of the subordinates' job potential and university ranking (competence) as a determinant of career progress. The quality of exchange was shown to mediate the relationship between competence and career progress. It is interesting to note that liking has been found to be a significant predictor of LMX (Dockery & Steiner, 1990; Wayne & Ferris, 1990).

Lowin and Craig (1968) documented that leaders showed more warmth and support towards competent subordinates. Kim and Organ (1982), in a more direct test with the experimental setting of MBA students, discovered that subordinate competence was a very strong determinant of the quality of exchange. In a replication of the same study for the social service organizations, the findings were validated (Snyder & Bruning, 1985). The findings can well be explained in terms of the social exchange theory (Blau, 1964) as per the model. Since the leader, according to the theorization, is interested in collaboration on unstructured tasks, and complex tasks, he or she is interested in the member's relevant skills. Competence in the exchange framework is the input from the subordinate which is a valued resource for the leader.

As we have noted earlier, the development of leader–member exchanges is rooted in the role-making process for unstructured tasks. Therefore, variables related to roles and nature of task should be potentially fruitful determinants. Kim and Organ (1982) also studied the statistical interaction between subordinate competence and task stress. The analysis indicated that, for high stress jobs, the leader initiated better quality of exchanges with competent subordinates. Snyder and Bruning (1985), in their replication study, took role conflict and role clarity, instead of task stress, along with competence. The interaction hypothesis was not significant either for role conflict or for role clarity. In this study, the measures of role conflict and clarity were taken both from the leader and the subordinate perspectives. In the final analysis, both were averaged to give one score to each variable. This probably led to the discrepancy in the results.

The studies mentioned above tested the subordinate characteristics either independently or along with task variables (e.g., role stress). The compatibility hypothesis mentioned at the outset remains to be investigated. Duchon, Green, and Taber (1986) tried to see a match between some demographic variables of the leaders and the members. The test was not a one-to-one match of the leader and the member. The results showed that most of the people who were a part of the IN-Group were females and belonged to higher class status (i.e., college juniors or seniors as opposed to freshmen or sophomores). The parallel analysis for the leaders revealed that all the leaders had higher class status and 31 of the 49 leaders were females. The results fit into the similarity proposition. All the same, it is only an indirect test of the compatibility hypothesis.

The empirical evidence testing the antecedent conditions is, indeed, very meager. Relevant dimensions need to be mapped to test the 'compatibility hypothesis' as this would lead to an understanding in the exchange framework. Also, the variable of climate that has been found effective in the leadership area (e.g., Baumgartel, 1981; Likert, 1967; Litwin & Stringer, 1968) needs to be studied.

Consequences of LMX

Almost all the leadership theorizations have aimed at predicting outcome variables. The outcomes have been mostly for the members. As pointed out earlier in this chapter, all the previous average theories (ALS) attempted to predict the outcomes for the workgroup.

The VDL theorization, by its very nature, evaluates the outcomes for the subordinates individually. What follows is a brief review of the outcome variables explained or attempted to be explained by the VDL theorization.

The VDL approach contends that since members have differing exchanges with their leader, their job-related experiences and behaviors too are different. Satisfaction of the members is the most widely investigated variable in terms of leadership. To some extent, it is a measure of the leader effectiveness. Satisfaction, in this framework, should be more for the IN-Group members than for the OUT-Group members. In other words, the quality of exchange should be positively related to satisfaction. This is a hypothesis that has received enormous support from the data (Dansereau et al., 1975; Vecchio & Gobdel, 1984). Graen and Ginsburgh (1977) also reported that the quality of exchange (measured in terms of leader acceptance) and role orientation (match between the job characteristics and the work interests of the workers) jointly determined the member's job satisfaction. Scandura and Graen (1984) found that leadership intervention based on the LMX assumptions showed an improvement in the satisfaction of OUT-Group members. This was evaluated by comparing satisfaction of the members before and after the intervention.

A related concept of felt (in)equity by the members has also been explored. Results show that whereas the members with a high quality of exchange do not perceive inequity in their leader's behaviors, those with low quality of exchanges do (Vecchio, Griffeth, & Hom, 1986).

It has been recommended that the turnover of the employees be studied in terms of leadership (Krackhardt, Mckenna, Porter, & Steers, 1981). But, with a few exceptions (e.g., ibid.), turnover research has been mainly studied in terms of satisfaction (Graen et al., 1982). Although some researches have shown a negative correlation between LMX quality and intention to quit (Major, Kozlowski, Chao & Gardner, 1995; Sparrowe, 1994; Vecchio and Gobdel, 1984; Wilhelm, Herd, & Steiner, 1993), research is impoverished in the area of actual turnover. Hence, there is a need for a shift in the focus of attention to leadership phenomenon to explain employee turnover.

Graen and Ginsburgh (1977) showed that quality of exchange and role acceptance interacting together predicted employee turnover. Graen et al. (1982) found LMX to be a better predictor of turnover than ALS—a finding that was replicated successfully in one study (Ferris, 1985) but failed to receive support in the other (Vecchio, 1985). The LMX theorization did not predict turnover in some other studies as well (e.g., Vecchio & Gobdel, 1984; Vecchio et al., 1986). Organizational citizenship behaviors, i.e., the behaviors that are beneficial to the organization and may go beyond the expected/formal employment contract too have been shown to be positively related to the quality of exchange (Wayne & Green, 1993).

As to the performance of the subordinates, the findings are mixed. Whereas some studies have found support for the LMX model (e.g., Scandura & Graen, 1984, Seers & Graen, 1984), others have failed to do so (e.g., Vecchio, 1982). The performance rated by the leader found support, whereas objective measures of performance did not.

Career progress of the members is another variable that occupies a central position in the VDL model. To study the career progress of the managers, a longitudinal study was initiated in Japan in 1972.

Wakabayashi and Graen (1984) reported that a seven-year follow-up showed that the career progress of the members was a function not only of their competence but also of the initial quality of exchange with their leader. This finding received support later in a 13-year follow-up study also (Wakabayashi, Graen, Graen, & Graen, 1988). The LMX has also been shown to have a positive correlation with performance appraisal (Duarte, Goodson, & Klich, 1994, Liden, Sparrow, & Wayne, 1997).

Other results also show that the IN/OUT-Group members differ in terms of their perception of the climate (Kozlowski & Doherty, 1989), job-related problems, psychological value of their work (Dansereau et al., 1975), congruence between their present and desired roles (Graen & Schiemann, 1978), affective commitment (Schriesheim, Neider, Scandura, & Tepper, 1992), perceived organizational support (Wayne, Shore, & Liden, 1997) and influence in decision-making (Scandura, Graen, & Novak, 1986).

Thus, in retrospect, although research on outcomes does provide support to the VDL predictions, there is also evidence against the theorization. As Greenwald (1975) points out, if the conflicting results are not attributable to some obvious statistical artifact or other cause, theoretically they need to be justified.

One probable cause of this fluctuation is the predictor measure. The LMX measure has been variable in all the studies and this probably led to the differing results. Thus, renewed efforts need to be made with strong and stable measures of the quality of exchange.

Extensions of the Model

The dyadic model has seen a few extensions to incorporate other related organizational phenomena. The main objective here is to explain global organizational dynamics.

Likert (1961) proposed that, for an organization, it was not enough to have effective units working independently. Organizations are effective on the whole only if these units are linked through a process of mutual influence. His theorization clearly focused on intra-unit effectiveness. The leader of a group is the connecting link, as he or she happens to be a member or subordinate of another group. Cashman, Dansereau, Graen, and Haga (1976) borrowed this notion in their formulation. They had two concepts. One was of course the concept of the leader's exchanges with his or her members (VDL). This they called intra-unit differentiation. As an additional measure, they took inter-unit differentiation which was the standing of the leader vis-à-vis his or her own supervisor. Thus a leader could be in his or her superior's IN or OUT group too. Their analysis showed that the job problems (of the members) relating to work were predicted by inter-unit differentiation and, the job problems (of the members) concerning relationship were predicted more by intra-unit differentiation. Thus, for the members in a work-group, there are linkages which are beyond their control but which have an impact upon their organizational experiences. The quality of linking pin (inter-unit differentiation) of the leaders determines work experience and satisfaction of the subordinates (Graen, Cashman, Ginsburgh, & Schiemann, 1977).

In another extension, the quality of exchange was taken in conjunction with the role orientation. Graen, Orris, and Johnson (1973) suggested that these two dimensions on the job were important for the subsystem functioning. The second dimension of role orientation concerns itself with the work. Specifically, it is a match between the work interests of the members and the characteristics of the task. Thus these two dimensions together determine outcomes, like job performance and job resignation for the members. The joint effect of the two was also shown to influence productivity and performance of the subordinates (Graen, Novak, & Sommerkamp, 1982).

Seers and Graen (1984) redefined the model. The concept of role orientation was replaced with the job characteristics model (Hackman & Oldham, 1976). The dual-attachment model given by Seers and Graen (1984) is a hybrid of LMX and job characteristics models.

This extension of the model stresses upon the interactive importance of interpersonal and technical characteristics. Since they are matched for individuals, they take care of individual needs also.

The VDL theorization in both these extensions is very sound. But there is little empirical evidence to support the extensions. The two aspects of work and people are aptly considered in the dual-attachment model. Whereas the earlier Average Leadership Styles identified these two dimensions, they were basically interpersonal in nature, as both were a part of leader behavior. The dual-attachment model takes care of the two aspects in their pure form. This might be a very useful notion for future leadership research.

The Present Research

To enumerate the objectives of the present research we go back to the theoretical model of role development by the members. One way to test the developmental aspect of the model is through longitudinal studies. This would show how a particular quality of exchange develops. But the stability of the quality of exchange, once it has been crystallized, has been documented well. Thus, one can safely conduct a cross-sectional study at this stage.

To begin with we enter the organization at one cross-section of time and take only those interactions that have had considerable time to crystallize. Thus, one can study the dyadic exchanges in terms of the model presented. If at the time of entry the relationship in the dyad has stabilized, it means that the role routinization phase is over. The relationship at this stage has both the behavioral and the qualitative aspects. The behavioral elements would involve work behavior of both the leader and the member. This aspect would follow the exchange process to some aspect. It is likely that the leader might be giving more latitude and freedom to some subordinates in return for their increased effort and involvement on the job. The relational aspects do not necessarily follow the exchanges overtly. They will tap the various dimensions of the quality of relationship from both the leader and the member perspectives.

Thus, the first objective of the present study is to develop a multidimensional measure that incorporates the qualitative as well as the behavioral aspects of the leader–member interactions. The measures have to be such that they can be evaluated both by the leader and the members. Different dimensions of quality of interaction have to be taken. The details of the conceptualization and specific objectives have been discussed in Chapter 3.

Once the quality of interaction has been identified, one goes back to see what could have been the possible variables that led to the present quality of exchange. To answer this question, we essentially turn to the first evaluative phase of role taking by the members. At this stage, the leader is identifying the relevant skills and orientations of the members. The relevance of the orientations of the member is in terms of either the leader's own orientation or in terms of the working atmosphere (climate) created by the leader.

The compatibility of the leader characteristics and those of the member can be understood in the exchange framework also. The leader evaluates the member keeping in view the exchanges that are to follow. Thus, the personal orientations of the leader and those of the member also follow the exchange rules. For example, if the leader is power oriented, he or she will look for a subordinate who is less independent and show more dependence on the leader. The leader's power orientation is a valued outcome for the member and the member's dependence is a valued outcome for the leader. For some characteristics, like achievement orientation, it might follow the similarity rule in the exchange framework. The same line of reasoning applies to a test of compatibility between the individual characteristics and those of the organization (i.e., climate). Thus, the next part of the research aims to study some antecedent variables and test the compatibility of these variables for the leaders and the members. These variables are the leader characteristics, member characteristics, leader's perceived climate, and the member's perceived climate. Specific hypotheses are stated in Chapter 4.

Finally, the study aims to examine some outcomes for the members. This is where the predictive utility of the model lies. In the second stage of role making, we identified some resources that the leader provides to the members. The resources are the outcomes for the members, but they are a part of the exchange. However, these are not the outcomes that we are interested in. For this reason, we make a distinction between the types of outcomes. Besides the outcomes (e.g., latitude, attention, etc.), *in* the exchange process, there are some outcomes which are the result *of* the exchange process. Whereas the former outcomes are immediate and negotiated, the latter are not so immediate and are natural croppings of the exchange. We call the former outcomes *proximal* outcomes and the latter *distal* outcomes. In other words, proximal outcomes characterize the quality of exchange and the distal outcomes are a result of this quality exchange. For the present purposes, we are mainly interested in distal outcomes. We aim to see how satisfaction, commitment, intent to leave, and perception of unit effectiveness depend on the quality of exchange.

Another outcome, i.e., influence in dyads is a debatable concept. The amount or extent of influence has been taken as a proximal outcome and rightly so. The present research aims to study the actual use of influence strategies that the leaders and the members use to influence each other. This, definitely, is not a part of the exchange process. Thus, whereas the extent of influence is a proximal outcome, the actual use of influence strategies is a distal one. The objective here is to study the actual use of influence strategies by the leaders and the members as a function of quality of interaction. Specific hypotheses regarding the outcome variables are given in Chapter 5.

A summary of the proposed relationships is presented in Figure 1.2.

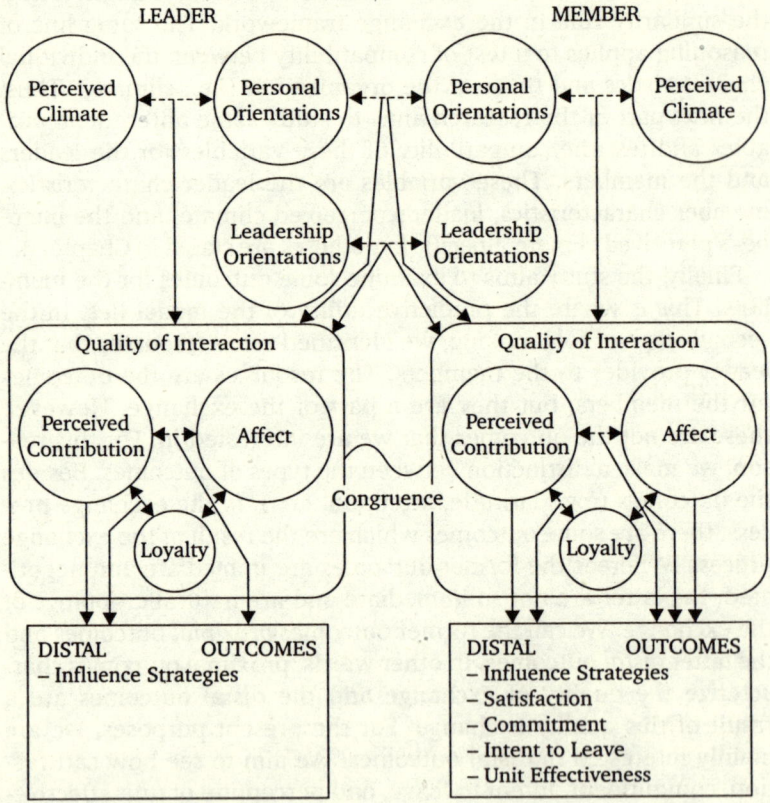

Figure 1.2: **Posited Relationships among Study Variables.**
Broken lines show interaction, solid lines show the effect of relationship.

◄ Chapter 2 ►

Investigation Strategies

An Overview

It is our belief that a theory or model should stand the test of empiricism for it to be valid. Hence, we subject our model to rigorous empirical analysis and all our contentions are based on the results of this analysis. The present work involves two studies conducted at two different times. In this chapter, the methodological details of the studies are explicated. The chapter is divided into two parts. Part one of the chapter contains the details of the first study. Data were collected from four organizations. The characteristic features of these organizations are given in the first section. Followed by this, the second section outlines the characteristics of the participants in terms of the leaders' and members' biographical data. The third section deals with the procedures adopted in the study. Finally, the fourth section describes the psychometric properties of the measures employed in the study.

The second part of the chapter deals with the details of the second study and is modeled exactly after the first part. This, too, has four sections showing the details of the organization, characteristics of the participants, the procedures followed, and the psychometric properties of the measures used, in the same order. However, the descriptions of the instruments do not follow the same pattern. As most of the measures in the second study were based on the factor structures of Study 1, the same analysis was not repeated in the second study. Also, the small sample size precludes this analysis.

First Investigation (Study 1)

Research Site

We conducted our study in four organizations located in northern India. No attempt was made to pick up the organizations randomly, as they differed from one another in many respects. One major factor that attracted us most was the ownership of the organizations. Keeping this in mind, we selected two private and two public sector organizations. Although all the organizations taken were production units, they were involved in the production of different goods ranging from urea to electrical equipments. A brief description of the organizations follows.

Synthetics Limited

This is a large, private sector organization owned and started by one of the biggest business houses in the country. It is the country's first synthetic fiber plant, set up in the early 1960s. Despite facing several difficulties and obstacles the company has continued to expand.

Presently, the company has 11 divisions located in different parts of the country: manufacturing nylon filament yarn, tyre cord, polyester filament yarn, polyester staple fiber, acrylic fiber, synthetic fiber machinery, grey and white cement, and other equipments. The data used here were collected from one of these divisions— i.e., Synthetic Fiber Machinery.

The Managing Director (MD), who is also the owner, is at the apex of the company. Below him are the two General Managers (GMs), under whom are several managers and assistant managers. But the managers of the personnel department and management information systems report directly to the MD. Below the managers are the trainees and/or supervisors. In all, the company employs around 4,000 people, of which around 80 belong to the executive level. The organization takes care of the needs and problems of its employees.

On the whole, the organization is effective both financially and otherwise. Strikes, lockouts, etc. are rare showing the psychological well-being of the employees. Different sections of the division such as sales, finance, and accounts, were sampled for the present study. The data were collected from all levels of management ranging from the GMs to the supervisors.

Urea Limited

This is a public limited concern, but privately owned. It is affiliated to a parent company in the United Kingdom. Established in the 1960s, this organization is now in an intensely competitive situation, with the availability exceeding the demand. Mainly a urea plant, it works at 95 percent capacity.

The other business sectors of this organization deal with explosives, paints, polyethene, rubber chemical, pharmaceuticals, and polyester staple fiber.

A Chief Executive (CE) heads the urea production unit. The CE is assisted by GM, GM (Works), and a Finance Manager. The Works Operation Manager, Chief Engineer, and Senior Personnel Manager report to the GM (Works). The Deputy Superintendents and the staff assist managers. The organization employs a 1,720 strong work-force, of which around 280 belong to the managerial and supervisory levels.

The organization has a reputation of giving a lot of benefits to its employees. The overtime rates are very high and the executives are very well paid. The company takes good care of the needs of the workers. It has sophisticated instruments and a good working environment.

One characteristic feature is the presence of employee unions of the non-managerial staff. There are three unions: an employee union, a fertilizers union, and a mazdoor union. The unions are strong and strikes and lockouts are frequent. Managers and executives from the top-most level to the supervisory level from the various units of the organization were sampled for the study.

Power Limited

This is a public sector organization set up in the late 1950s involved in the production of power plant equipments. It manufactures a gamut of equipment for thermal, hydro, and nuclear power plants. The range includes products and systems for power generation, transmission, and utilization. The work ranges from manufacturing individual equipment to setting up power plants on a turnkey basis.

The company has 13 manufacturing plants situated in different parts of the country. These individual plants have unique manufacturing and testing facilities. The sophisticated facilities at the organization are state-of-the-art in the manufacturing processes.

The company is headed by the Chairman-cum-Managing Director (MD) who is also a member of the Board of Directors. Under the Chairman are the different Directors and Executive Directors.

Technical, Finance, Personnel, and Production divisions have corporate functions (such as research and development, finance, taxation, and human resources management). A Director who reports to the MD leads each division. The Power and the Industrial systems divisions are business sectors and are led by a Director each, who also reports to the MD. Finally Executive Directors, who also report to the MD, lead the different operating units. The organization has a vast reservoir of manufacturing skills and management. It employs around 7,500 employees, with around 700 executives. Data for the study were collected from the corporate office of the organization located in a metropolitan city of the country. The respondents in this organization were high-level managers, mainly Deputy General Managers and Senior Managers.

Woolen Mills

This is now a public sector organization. It has had a long history. A Britisher under a different name started it in 1896. With mergers over a period of time, the company became a part of a bigger corporate. In 1937, for the first time, three Indians appeared on the Board of Directors. In 1955, the ownership was transferred to an Indian industrialist. In 1962, another business family took over. In 1970, part of the big corporation was taken over by the Government; and in 1981, the woolen mills too became a public sector organization. The organization manufactures woolen goods like blankets, suit lengths, and shawls.

This company is one of the four subsidiaries of the larger corporation. It is headed by a GM. The senior managerial positions are the posts of Managers and Assistant Managers in the administration. On the production side, there are different Chief Engineers of dying, loom, etc. The assistant Chief Engineers, senior engineers, plant engineers, and supervisors follow the hierarchy in the same order. The company employs around 3,300 employees, of which around 250 serve at different managerial levels. Managers from different levels representing different units participated in the study.

Procedure

The data were collected with the help of a structured questionnaire. After seeking entry into the organization, the organizational chart was obtained. All such managers were approached who had at least four people reporting directly to them. These managers were treated as the leaders. The members randomly chosen reporting to leaders were treated as the subordinates. This sampling frame provided leaders an opportunity to evaluate their immediate subordinates, and subordinates to evaluate their immediate leaders.

The first section of the questionnaire (see Appendix I) contained 'Quality of Interaction' and 'Influence Strategy' measures. These two measures tapped the interaction between the leader and the individual subordinates. Hence, the leader responded to these two measures for all the subordinates chosen under him (two to four). Similarly, all the members (chosen) under a leader evaluated their interaction with their leader. Thus, if one leader had four subordinates under him, he responded to the two measures for all the four subordinates separately (four times). On the other hand, each of the four members evaluated his leader once. This was done because the objective was to see the dyadic interaction (between a leader and a member) on these two measures. The other sections were related to individual dispositions, perceptions, and behaviors and, hence, were filled up once by each respondent. Thus for the sections of quality of exchange and influence strategies the N was 304, and for the other sections, the N was 219. It took approximately 10 to 15 minutes to complete the first section and around 30 to 35 minutes to complete the rest of the questionnaire.

In the beginning, the aim was to take up one leader and four (sometimes three) members under him. In Synthetics Limited, thus, one leader evaluated his interaction generally with four members. In the course of data collection, it was realized that obtaining so much information from one individual (the leader) had some practical difficulties. Among others was the time constraint. Hence, for the next three organizations, the number of subordinates under a leader was limited to two. That is, one leader gave information on the first section for two members, separately.

Participants

Altogether 219 executives from the aforementioned four diverse organizations constituted the sample for Study 1. Almost all the respondents were male (except three). The participants were taken from the different divisions of the organizations like production, accounts, sales, and personnel.

As will be made clear in the next section, the two perspectives— the leader and the member—were of prime concern for the present investigations. Therefore, a split of the sample, in terms of these two perspectives, is imperative. The organization-wise split—the total respondents, number of leaders, and number of members—is given in Table 2.1.

Table 2.1
Organization-wise Split of the Respondents (Study 1)

	Leaders	Members	Total
Synthetics Limited	11	40	51
Urea Limited	15	30	45
Power Limited	15	30	45
Woolen Mills	26	52	78
Total	67	152	219

Of the 219 respondents, 67 (30.59 percent) were leaders and 152 (69.41 percent) were members. Table 2.2 depicts the mean scores on background characteristics of the participants. It can be seen that the leaders had significantly higher scores than the members on age, educational qualifications, tenure in the organization, and number of promotions received. However, leaders and members were not significantly different in tenure in the present position.

Table 2.2

Means and F-ratios of Background Variables for Leaders and Members (Study 1)

Variables	Means			
	Leader (n = 67)	Member (n = 152)	F(1, 217)	Overall Means (N = 219)
Age	48.09	41.00	49.41[a]	43.17
Qualification*	1.50	1.12	20.40[a]	1.24
Number of Years in the Organization	16.81	13.63	8.31[a]	14.60
Number of Years in the Present Position	3.63	3.20	1.89	3.33
Number of Promotions	4.21	2.95	25.88[a]	3.33

Note: [a] $p < .01$; *3-point scale.

Table 2.3 shows the percentage distributions of the leaders and members on background information. So far as the age of the respondents is concerned, leaders showed less variation, with no leader below the age of 30; the bulk of them were in the age range of 45 to 49 years (47.8 percent). On the other hand, the analysis showed a greater variation for members in age; the youngest member was 23 years old and most of them were in the age range of 35 to 49 years (71.1 percent). The same was true of educational qualifications. All the leaders were at least graduates and none of them had a qualification below that. The majority (86.6 percent) of the leaders had a masters or an equivalent degree. Here also the members showed more variability. A few of them (5.9 percent) were not even graduates and the rest were distributed over the other two categories. Leaders had had a longer tenure in the organization; most of them had their stay in the organization from 10 to 29 years (83.6 percent). Most of the members (74.4 percent) had tenure ranging from one to 19 years. The tenure in the present position of both the leaders and members was mostly one to four years. Forty-eight (71.6 percent) leaders and 119 (78.2 percent) members had been in the present position for the above mentioned duration. Most of the leaders (80.6 percent) had received three to six promotions, whereas most members (76.9 percent) had received one to four promotions only.

Table 2.3
Percentage Distribution of Respondents—Leaders and Members—on Background Variables (Study 1)

Variable	Leader (n = 67)	Member (n = 152)	Overall (N = 219)
Age (in Years)			
29 or below	0.0	10.5	7.3
30 to 34	1.5	12.9	5.0
35 to 39	6.0	20.1	16.4
40 to 44	13.4	24.6	23.3
45 to 49	47.8	21.4	30.1
50 to 54	19.4	9.2	12.3
55 and above	11.9	2.6	5.5
Qualification			
Below Graduation	0.0	5.9	4.1
Graduation	13.4	37.5	30.1
Masters'	86.6	56.6	65.8
Tenure in Organization (in Years)			
4 or less	6.0	13.8	11.4
5 to 9	8.9	13.2	11.9
10 to 14	23.9	29.6	27.8
15 to 19	20.9	17.8	18.7
20 to 24	19.4	15.1	16.4
25 or more	20.9	10.5	13.7
Tenure in Present Position (in Years)			
2 or less	35.8	46.0	42.9
3 to 4	35.8	32.2	33.3
5 to 6	17.9	12.5	14.1
7 to 8	6.0	4.6	5.0
9 or more	4.5	4.6	4.6
Number of Promotions			
None	6.0	5.9	5.0
1 to 2	7.5	33.5	25.6
3 to 4	37.3	43.4	37.0
5 to 6	43.3	14.5	23.3
7 to 8	6.0	2.6	3.6

Obviously, the two samples—leaders and members—were significantly different from each other in terms of background characteristics.

Measures

To test the model in general, and specific hypotheses in particular, a questionnaire was prepared which consisted of various tests and measures. Most of the measures were taken from the existing published literature. The questionnaire was divided into five sections (see Appendix I). Section I contained items on quality of exchange and influence strategies. Sections II and III contained items on personal attributes and perceived climate, respectively. Section IV comprised outcome variables—satisfaction and commitment. Finally, Section V contained biographical information and intent to leave items.

At the outset, almost all the measures were subjected to a varimax rotated principal components analysis (Nie, Hull, Jenkins, Steinbrenner, & Bent, 1975). Nie et al. (1975) have described five methods of factoring. Of which, the two most common methods are: Principal Factoring *without* Iteration (PAI) and Principal Factoring *with* Iteration (PA2). In the present study, all the measures were analyzed using the latter method. This was done for two reasons. First, it automatically replaces the main diagonal elements of the correlation matrix with communality estimates, thereby automatically giving the so-called inferred factor. Second, it employs an iteration procedure for improving the communality estimates. The varimax rotation emphasizes cleaning up the factors rather than variables.

The items and the factors retained, following the factor analysis results, were selected on the following two criteria. Only those factors were retained that had an eigenvalue generally greater than or equal to 1.00. Then, within a factor only those items were taken that had a factor loading greater than or equal to .30 on the defining component and cross-loading generally less than or equal to .25. Those items that loaded heavily on more than one factor were included in all the factors that they loaded on. The measures used in the study is discussed in the following sections.

Quality of Exchange (QEX)

Leader–Member Exchange (LMX) Measure

One of the measures used is the five-item version of the Leader–Member Exchange Scale (Graen, Liden, & Hoel, 1982). The responses were taken only from the subordinates wherein they evaluated their immediate supervisor (leader). Thus, the number of respondent for this measure was 152. The factor analysis results of the five items yielded one clear factor. The five items showed factor loading of .25, .57, .55, .34, and .74. The scale documented a fairly high reliability coefficient of .81. The M and SD of the scale were 14.81 and 3.30, respectively.

Quality of Interaction (QI)

The present research is centered round the construct of 'quality of exchange.' Thus a new measure—'Quality of interaction' scale—was developed to measure the quality of exchange between a leader and a member. Because of the centrality of this construct in the present research, it has been given a detailed treatment in Chapter 3.

Personal Orientations (PO)

The Manifest Need Questionnaire (MNQ) developed by Steers and Braunstein (1976) was used to measure the personal needs. This instrument is designed to measure four needs—Achievement, Affiliation, Autonomy, and Dominance—through behaviorally based items with specific reference to work settings.

The scale consisted of 20 items, with five items in each of the four subscales. Five items were reverse-scored. The respondents were asked to rate on a seven point scale (*1 = never; 7 = always*) as to how *frequently* each of the statements most accurately described their behavior at work.

Since the psychometric properties of the subscales are not available in the Indian setting, it was considered appropriate to run a varimax rotated principal components analysis on the item responses. While performing this statistical analysis, some additional data were provided by Lakhtakia (1990), thus making an $N = 444$. The analysis yielded three neat and meaningful factors explaining a total of 78.2 percent of the variance. The three factors that emerged were named Achievement (PA), Independence (PI), and Power (PP). The fourth factor of relationship did not emerge as an independent configuration. Factor loadings obtained are presented in Table 2.4.

Table 2.5 presents the descriptive statistics, intercorrelations, and reliability coefficients of the subscales. The factors exhibited reliability levels well above .50 as a minimum level for acceptable

Table 2.4

Factor Loadings Obtained—Personal Orientation Measures
(N = 444)

Items		Achievement	Independence	Power
10.	I try very hard to improve on my past performance	.60	.01	.05
11.	I try to avoid any added responsibilities on my job	.39	−.28	.02
14.	I do my best work when job assignments are fairly difficult	.53	.13	.02
16.	I try to perform better than my co-workers	.59	.10	.19
17.	I strive to gain more control over the events around me	.46	.07	.41
2.	I go my own way regardless of the opinion of others	.06	.44	.13
5.	In my work assignments, I try to be my own boss	.16	.33	.34
7.	I disregard rules and regulations that hamper my personal freedom	−.06	.46	.05
8.	I try my best to work alone on a job	.12	.67	.06
3.	I strive to be in command when I am working in a group	.04	.17	.75
6.	I seek an active role in the leadership of a group	.21	.04	.46
Eigenvalue		3.05	.61	.99
Percentage of Variance		42.20	22.30	13.70

Table 2.5
Descriptive Statistics, Reliabilities, and Intercorrelations of Personal Orientation Measures (Study 1)

		1	2	3	M	SD	Alpha
					(N = 444)		
1.	Achievement	x	32	56	27.8	4.2	66
2.	Independence	17	x	49	14.8	4.4	59
3.	Power	52	44	x	19.8	3.9	67
	M (N = 219)	28.3	15.6	19.7			
	SD	3.9	4.4	4.0			
	Alpha	70	64	69			
	No. Items	5	4	4			

Note: Decimal points in correlation matrix and alpha are omitted; correlations below the diagonal are for combined data ($N = 444$) for which required rs are .10 and .12 at $p < .05$ and $p < .01$, respectively; correlations above the diagonal are for the present sample ($N = 219$) for which required rs are .14 and .18 at $p < .05$ and $p < .01$, respectively.

reliability (Nunnally, 1978). The correlations among the factors ranged from .17 to .52, with an average correlation of .37.

For the present sample too, the reliability coefficients are well above the cut-off mark. The intercorrelations range from .32 to .56 (average $r = .46$), showing a fair amount of scale independence.

Relationship did not emerge as an independent factor. It has been reported that affiliation gets in the way of effective management (McClelland & Winter, 1969). Thus, it is probable that relationship is more of a variable behavioral dimension (as relationship-oriented leader behavior). As a personal need probably it is not very relevant to work situations. Also, as the Indian society is considered to be a collectivist society (Hofstede, 1980), affiliation is probably more of a meta-value and less of a personal orientation.

Organizational Climate (OC)

The concept of climate undoubtedly has been proved very useful, but at the same time it has evoked tremendous controversies. Unit of analysis is one major issue. The question is whether one is measuring psychological (perceived) climate or the attributes of the organization as a whole (structural or objective climate). The unit of analysis forms the perceptual and structural approaches to the study of climate (Ansari, 1980; Ansari, Baumgartel, & Sullivan, 1982). Whereas some (e.g., Guion, 1973; James & Jones, 1974) question the validity of perceptual measures, others (e.g., Hellreigel & Slocum, 1974) favor them on the ground that objective characteristics only indirectly influence the organizational participants. For the present purpose, the psychological climate, which is the individual perception of the members of the organization, is of interest.

The MNQ (Steers & Braunstein, 1976) was modified to represent the climate (or presses) of the organization. Since the aim was to see a *match* between the personal orientations of the members and their perception of the climate, the climate measures were modified to reveal the equivalent presses of the organization. The scale consisted of 20 items (see the previous section for details). The respondents were asked to evaluate on a seven-point scale (*1 = to almost no extent*; *7 = to a very great extent*) the *extent* to which each item was true to their organization.

Before subjecting the data to a factor analysis, additional data were taken from Lakhtakia (1990), making the $N = 444$. The analysis constrained to three interpretable factors, explaining a total of 94.7 percent of the variance. The factor loadings obtained are reported in Table 2.6.

Table 2.6
Factor Loadings Obtained—Organizational Climate Measures
(N = 444)

Items	Achievement	Independence	Power
22. In this organization there is a feeling of pressure to continually improve individual and group performance	.50	.11	.18
27. This organization stimulates and approves of innovation and experimentation	.74	.27	.03
28. In this organization we set fairly high standards for performance	.67	.25	.21

Table 2.6 continued

Table 2.6 continued

Items	Achievement	Independence	Power
30. In this organization, it is up to us to decide how our job should best be done	.17	.67	.12
35. In this organization, we are free to set our performance goal	.20	.70	.09
36. In this organization, there are opportunities for independent thoughts and action on our job	.31	.74	.10
38. In this organization, we have a great deal of freedom to decide how we do our job	.19	.82	-.02
29. This organization prefers to be its own boss, even where it needs assistance, or where a joint effort is needed	.01	.06	.58
32. Status symbols are especially important for this organization and it uses them to gain influence over others	.04	.02	.57
40. This organization provides a lot of power and control to upper-level management	.14	.13	.30
Eigenvalue	6.33	1.31	0.94
Percentage of Variance	69.80	14.50	10.40

The first factor, *Achievement* (CA), contained items dealing with the standards of performance and the pressure put by the organization to meet those demands. The second factor, *Independence* (CI), contained items showing the opportunities provided for independent thoughts and actions by the organization and the freedom on the job. The third dimension, *Power* (CP), contained items showing the degree of power yielded by the organization over the individual members. They specifically rated the extent to which the organization controlled and directed the activities of the members.

Table 2.7 shows the descriptive statistics and reliability coefficients of and intercorrelations among the three factors for combined data ($N = 444$) as well as the equivalent statistics for the data of the present study ($N = 219$). It can be seen that the reliability of the third factor, Power, is just below the required level for the combined data ($N = 444$); however, it touches the acceptability mark of .50 for the data of the present study. The intercorrelations among the factors are substantially low (average $r = .26, N = 219$), indicating a reasonable amount of scale independence.

Table 2.7
Descriptive Statistics, Reliabilities, and Intercorrelations of Climate Measures (Study 1)

		1	2	3	M (N = 444)	SD	Alpha
1.	Achievement	x	46	25	13.9	3.9	84
2.	Independence	45	x	07	17.7	5.4	88
3.	Power	14	03	x	14.2	3.1	50
	M(N = 219)	13.2	16.4	13.6			
	SD	3.7	5.6	3.4			
	Alpha	73	85	47			
	No. Items	3	5	3			

Note: Decimal points in correlation matrix and alpha are omitted; correlations below the diagonal are for the combined data ($N = 444$) for which required rs are .10 and .12 at $p < .05$ and $p < .01$, respectively; correlations above the diagonal are for the present sample for which required rs are .14 and .18 at $p < .05$ and $p < .01$, respectively.

For climate too, relationship did not emerge as an independent factor. Since MNQ has been modified to represent climate, this failure too is probably because of the same reason as for personal orientations.

Influence Strategies (IN)

Forty-seven single-statement items were drawn from the available literature (Ansari, 1990; Falbo, 1977; Falbo & Peplau, 1980; Kipnis, Schmidt, & Wilkinson, 1980) to tap the respondents' upward and downward influence strategies. The respondents rated each item on a seven-point scale (*1 = never*; *7 = always*) estimating the *frequency* with which they used it to influence the target person (identified as immediate superior/subordinate) at work.

The analysis of the combined data—from *both* leader and member perspectives ($N = 304$)—disclosed five common factors (Table 2.8). A total of 84.1 percent of the variance was accounted for by the 24 significant items in the factor matrix. The extracted factors are described in the following sections.

Table 2.8
Factor Loadings Obtained—Influence Strategy Measures
(N = 304, Study 1)

Items	Factor				
	1	2	3	4	5
1. Call a staff meeting to back your request	.46	.21	.04	.07	.09
20. Obtain informal support of higher ups	.67	.26	.10	.16	.11
26. Bring some friends along to back your request	.53	.11	.01	.21	.07
30. Get the support of some higher up to back your request	.81	.06	.03	.24	.05
35. Get everyone else to agree with you before you make the request	.54	.29	.03	.13	.14
39. Refer the matter to higher authority if the situation so demands	.64	.20	-.07	.12	.20
3. Praise him/her with superlatives	.15	.62	.15	.07	.13
7. Get your way by making him/her feel that it was his/her idea	.16	.64	.06	.24	.12
19. Make him/her feel important	.09	.84	.03	.14	.05
27. Even when you know you would not use his/her idea you consult him/her	.24	.47	.03	.10	.08
32. Use the words that make him/her feel important	.16	.78	.02	.06	.10
11. Offer an exchange of favor	.02	.17	.78	.11	.07
13. Do a personal favor for him	.07	.03	.79	.00	.13
22. Help him/her even in personal matters	.02	.32	.62	.06	.17
24. Remind him/her of past favor you did for him/her	.19	.28	.64	.20	.03
36. Remind him/her how hard you had worked and it will only be fair for him/her to help you now	.27	.11	.42	.13	.02

Table 2.8 continued

Table 2.8 continued

44. Offer some personal sacrifice in exchange (e.g., doing part of his/her or others' job, etc.)	.04	.05	*.75*	.06	.18
8. Repeatedly ask him/her until he/she gives in	.22	.08	.13	*.77*	.03
28. Repeatedly persuade him/her to comply with your arguments as they are the need of the time	.15	.08	.14	*.59*	.25
47. Go on asking persistently till he/she does what you want	.29	.11	.06	*.65*	.04
21. Sometimes tell him/her the reasons for making the request	.08	.09	.21	.03	*.76*
31. Tell exactly why you need his/her help	.10	−.02	.11	−.03	*.73*
38. Tell him/her the reasons why your plan is the best	.13	.04	.28	.09	*.55*
41. Argue your points logically	.19	.07	.20	.07	*.59*
Eigenvalue	8.44	5.40	3.59	2.29	1.22
Percentage of Variance	33.9	21.7	14.40	9.20	4.90

Note: Factor 1 = Informal Support; Factor 2 = Ingratiation; Factor 3 = Personalized Exchange; Factor 4 = Persuasion; Factor 5 = Reasoning.

The first factor had the elements of support from friends, higher ups, and others. This was named *Informal Support* (IF). The second factor had the elements of flattery, praise, and making the target feel important. This was termed, *Ingratiation* (I). The third factor comprised personal favors on an exchange basis. Hence, this was labeled *Personalized Exchange* (PE). The fourth factor clearly contained items on persuading the target person. This was, therefore, named *Persuasion* (P). Finally, the last factor had rationality at the heart of all the items, and was called *Reasoning*.

The descriptive, statistics, reliability coefficients, and the intercorrelations of the subscales are given in Table 2.9. The reliabilities are substantially high and intercorrelations (average $r = .20$) substantially low, thereby showing reliable and sufficiently independent scales, respectively.

The factor analysis was repeated for the leader and the member separately. From the members' perspective, the same five dimensions emerged. However, from the leaders' perspective, two

Table 2.9
Descriptive Statistics, Reliabilities, and Intercorrelations of Influence Strategy Measures (Study 1)

	IES	I	PE	PR	R
IES	.80				
I	.39	.81			
PE	.15	.02	.84		
PR	.18	.08	.34	.78	
R	.42	.08	.29	.08	.81
Mean	15.46	17.39	17.32	10.25	20.70
SD	6.52	6.35	7.56	3.72	4.20
No. Items	6	5	6	3	4

Note: $r(302) = .11$ at $p < .05$; $r(302) = .15$ at $p < .01$; IS = Informal Support; I = Ingratiation; PE = Personalized Exchange; P = Persuasion; R = Reasoning. Diagonal entries indicate coefficients alpha.

additional factors—*Assertion* (A) and *Showing Expertise* (SE)—were obtained. Descriptive Statistics (*M* and *SD*), reliability coefficients, and number of items for the leader and member data are given in Table 2.10.

Table 2.10
Scale Characteristics and Reliability Coefficients of Influence Strategy Measures for Leaders and Members Separately

	Leader				Member			
	Alpha	M	SD	No. of Items	Alpha	M	SD	No. of Items
IS	.83	15.14	6.38	6	.80	15.46	6.52	6
I	.87	15.82	6.41	5	.81	17.39	6.35	5
PE	.86	18.35	7.73	6	.84	17.32	7.56	6
P	.79	10.67	3.69	3	.78	10.25	3.72	3
R	.84	20.54	4.36	4	.81	20.71	4.20	4
A	.54	8.14	2.29	2	–	–	–	–
SE	.84	26.68	5.85	5	–	–	–	–

Note: $N = 152$; IS = Informal Support; I = Ingratiation; PE = Personalized Exchange; P = Persuasion; R = Reasoning; A = Assertion; SE = Showing Expertise.

Satisfaction (SA)

A 16-item scale included satisfaction with different aspects of the job. The respondents were asked to indicate on a seven-point scale (*1 = very dissatisfied; 7 = very satisfied*) how *satisfied* they were with these aspects. A factor analysis yielded two neat factors. The results of the analysis are reported in Table 2.11. The two factors together explained 90.7 percent of the variance.

Table 2.11
Factor Loadings Obtained—Satisfaction Measures (N = 219, Study 1)

Items	Factor 1	Factor 2
2. The friendliness of the people you work with	.69	.18
5. The respect you receive from the people you work with	.67	.13
10. The amount of job security you have	.50	.24
11. The amount of personal growth and development you get in doing your job	.22	.77
12. The feeling of worthwhile accomplishment you get from doing your job	.31	.78
14. The amount of challenge in your job	.27	.72
16. The chances for advancement on your job	.06	.60
Eigenvalue	6.36	1.32
Percentage of Variance	75.10	15.60
M	16.38	18.45
SD	2.88	5.15

Note: $N = 219$; Factor 1 = Extrinsic Satisfaction; Factor 2 = Intrinsic Satisfaction.

The first factor had elements of friendliness, respect received, and job security, and was labeled, *Extrinsic Satisfaction* (ES). The second factor contained items reflecting the growth opportunity, challenge, and advancement on the job, and was called, *Intrinsic Satisfaction* (IS).

Extrinsic and Intrinsic satisfaction scales showed adequate reliability coefficients of .67 and .85, respectively, and were only moderately correlated ($r_{(217)} = .45$), revealing scale independence. The descriptive statistics (*M* and *SD*) of the two factors can be looked up in Table 2.11.

Commitment (CO)

The organizational commitment scale (Mott, 1972) originally consists of 15 items. The present study employed only nine items of this scale (including two negative ones). The six items that represented intent to leave dimension were left out, as this outcome dimension has received a separate treatment in the present research.

The respondents were asked to indicate on a seven-point scale (*1 = strongly disagree; 7 = strongly agree*) their *agreement/disagreement* with each item. A varimax rotated factor analysis yielded one single factor involving all the nine items, with factor loadings of .41, .68, .30, .64, .57, .33, .57, .34, and .43. The index of coefficient alpha was .87, with an M of 43.95 and a SD of 10.38.

Intent to Leave (IL)

Intent to leave was measured through a two-item scale (Mayes & Ganster, 1982). One item was positive and the other was reverse-scored. In both the items, the respondents were asked about their intention to leave or stay in the organization in the near future. The two items showed a very high correlation of .98. The scale had an M of 2.26 and a SD of .83.

Study 2

The data for the second study were collected with the main objective of studying the within-group variations from the subordinate perspective. In other words, the aim was to see whether different subordinates under one leader (a work-group) perceive the leader behavior differently. All the same, some of the hypotheses (e.g., interaction of leader's and member's personal attributes) were retested to check the validity of the Study 1 findings.

Only one organization was taken, as this study was an extension and validation of Study 1. Also, practical constraints of time precluded an employment of more organizations. In addition, all the measures used in the study were based on the factor analysis results of Study 1.

Research Site

Only one public sector organization, located in the north-eastern part of the country was taken. The details of the organization follow.

Fertilizer Division

This is a public sector organization established in 1963 and involved in the production of urea from naphtha. It has four divisions located in different parts of the country. All the divisions are involved in the production of fertilizer. The data were collected from one of the divisions of the organization.

This division is headed by a GM. The Deputy GM (administration) and the Deputy GM (factory) report to the GM. The Chief Engineers of different departments—technical services, civil, production, instruments, electrical, and mechanical—report to the Deputy GM (factory). Below the different Chief Engineers are the Additional Chief Engineers. Deputy Chief Engineers report to the Additional Chief Engineers. Assistant Chief Engineers report to the Additional Chief Engineers. Under the Assistant Chief Engineers are plant managers, assistant engineers, etc. Under the Deputy GM (administration) is a Chief Executive Officer (CEO). The Finance Manager, Chief Personnel Officer, Vigilance Officer, and the Chief Medical Officer all report to the CEO. These managers take care of their respective departments with the help of senior officers. The organization employs around 2,200 employees, with around 300 executives and managers. Managers and officers from the top-most level (Deputy GM) down to supervisors constituted the sample in the present study.

Procedure

As mentioned earlier, the data were collected only from one organization. The procedure of data collection was the same as in Study 1. From the organizational chart of the organization all such managers were taken who had at least four subordinates reporting to them. All the four subordinates under a leader were taken as the respondents.

The leaders gave their responses on the sections of personal attributes, perceived climate, self-reported leadership styles, and biographical information. The subordinates responded to all the sections of the questionnaire. Thus, for the measures of personal orientations, perceived climate, and biographical information, the N is 122 (both the leaders' and the subordinate responses); for the other sections, the N is 96 (only subordinates' responses). The self-reported leadership style measures were only taken from the leaders; hence, the N was 26 for this section.

Participants

In all 122 managers and executives from the aforementioned organization participated in the study. They belonged to different sections of administration and production (factory) units. Of the 122, 26 (21.31 percent) respondents were leaders and 96 (78.69 percent) were members.

Table 2.12 displays the mean scores of leaders, members, and total respondents on the background data. Leaders were significantly higher than the members on age, educational qualifications, and number of promotions received. However tenure in the organization and in present position did not reveal any significant differences.

Table 2.12

Means and F-ratios of Background Variables for Leaders and Members (Study 2)

Variables	Means			Overall Means
	Member (n = 96)	Leader (n = 26)	F (1,120)	(N = 122)
Age	47.06	50.38	9.20[a]	47.77
Qualification*	1.00	1.20	9.24[a]	1.06
Number of Years in the Organization	17.79	19.96	2.04	18.25
Number of Years in the Present Position	4.46	3.69	1.99	4.29
Number of Promotions	4.54	3.71	4.54[b]	4.36

Note: [a] $p < .01$; [b] $p < .05$; * 3-point scale.

Table 2.13 depicts the percentage distributions of leaders and members on the background data. In this sample, too, the leaders showed little variability on age with most of them (57.7 percent) falling in the range of 50 to 54 years and all of them in the range of 40 to 59 years. Members, on the other hand, were more variable on age, with 59.6 percent falling in the age range of 40 to 49 years. As regards educational qualifications, all the leaders had a masters or an equivalent degree. Among the members, 26 percent were graduates too. Most of the leaders (69.4 percent) had received three to six promotions, whereas most members (67.7 percent) had received one to four promotions.

Table 2.13

Percentage Distribution of Total Respondents—Leaders and Members—on Background Variables (Study 2)

Variable	Leader (n = 26)	Member (n = 96)	Overall (n = 122)
Age (in years)			
25–29	0.0	1.0	0.8
30–34	0.0	1.0	0.8
35–39	0.0	6.3	4.9
40–44	3.8	19.8	16.4
45–49	30.8	39.6	37.7
50–54	57.7	22.9	30.3
55–59	7.7	9.4	9.0
Qualification			
Below Graduation	0.0	2.1	1.6
Graduate	0.0	26.0	20.5
Master	100.0	71.9	77.9
Tenure in Organization (in years)			
4 or less	0.0	4.2	3.3
5–9	3.8	5.2	4.9
10–14	11.5	24.0	21.3
15–19	30.8	21.9	23.8
20–24	23.1	27.1	26.2
25–29	23.1	12.5	14.7
30 or more	7.7	5.2	5.7

Table 2.13 continued

Table 2.13 continued

Variable	Leader (n = 26)	Member (n = 96)	Overall (n = 122)
Tenure in Present Position (in years)			
3 or less	57.7	35.4	40.2
4 – 6	30.8	52.1	47.5
7 – 9	7.7	5.2	5.7
10 or more	3.8	7.2	6.6
Number of Promotions			
None	0.0	2.1	1.6
1 – 2	15.4	25.0	22.9
3 – 4	38.5	42.7	41.8
5 – 6	30.8	26.0	27.0
7 – 8	11.5	3.1	4.9
9 – 10	3.8	1.0	1.6

Measures

Most of the measures used in this study were taken directly from Study 1, with a few exceptions. The details of the questionnaire (see Appendix II) are as follows: Sections I and II contained items on personal attributes and perceived climate, respectively. The third section contained biographical information. The fourth section for the leaders had items of self-reported leadership styles; for the members, it contained style preference. Section V contained measures of quality of exchange taken from existing literature (in terms of Attention and Latitude). Section VI contained items of quality of interaction as measuring exchange. Finally, the seventh section contained the three outcome variables—satisfaction, commitment, and unit effectiveness.

The three factors—Achievement, Independence, and Power of **Personal Attributes** that emerged in the first study were taken in this study as it is. The reliability coefficients, M, SD, number of items, and intercorrelations among factors are given in Table 2.14. The reliability coefficients are fairly high and intercorrelations low enough.

Similarly, the three factors—Achievement, Independence, and Power of **Perceived Climate**—were also taken *a priori*. The scale characteristics, reliability coefficients, and intercorrelations can be

Table 2.14
Scale Characteristics, Coefficients Alpha, and Intercorrelations among Personal Orientation Measures (Study 2)

	PA	PI	PP
PA	.75		
PI	.08	.68	
PP	.43	.11	.80
Mean	26.79	17.63	14.60
SD	4.23	4.62	3.70
No. of items	5	4	2

Note: Diagonal entries indicate coefficients alpha; $N = 122$; $r(120) = .14$ at $p < .05$; $r(120) = .18$ at $p < .01$; PA, PI, and PP are Achievement, Independence, and Power orientations, respectively.

looked up in Table 2.15. As mentioned earlier, for both sections, the N was 122.

The self-reported **Leadership Style** (LS) was taken from Ansari (1990) and J.B.P. Sinha (1987). The three styles of leadership— Authoritarian (F), Participative (P), and Nurturant-task (NT)— were of interest and only items related to them were taken. The respondents were asked to evaluate on a seven-point scale (*1 = never, 7 = always*) how *frequently* each statement was true to them. Since the N for this section was very small (26), factor analysis was ruled out. The three styles—Authoritarian, Participative, and

Table 2.15
Scale Characteristics, Coefficients Alpha, and Intercorrelations among Climate Measures (Study 2)

	CA	CI	CP
CA	.76		
CI	.55	.87	
CP	.24	−.34	.51
Mean	11.69	15.44	13.93
SD	3.96	5.63	3.29
No. of items	3	4	3

Note: Diagonal entries indicate coefficients alpha; $N = 122$; $r(120) = .14$ at $p < .05$; $r(120) = .18$ at $p < .01$; CA, CI and, CP are Achievement, Independence, and Power Climate, respectively.

Nurturant-Task—were taken *a priori*. These three factors have been found to be important in the Indian setting. The relevant statistics are given in Table 2.16.

Table 2.16

Scale Characteristics, Coefficients Alpha, and Intercorrelations of Self-reported Leadership Style Measures

	LS(N)	*LS(P)*	*LS(F)*
LS(N)	.64		
LS(P)	.31	.77	
LS(F)	.22	−.03	.90
M	28.95	24.63	22.27
SD	4.31	5.79	7.26
No. of items	5	5	5

Note: Diagonal entries indicate coefficients alpha; r (24) = .39, at $p < .05$; r (24) = .50; $p < .01$; LS(N), LS(P), and LS(F) are, respectively, nurturant task, participative and authoritarian leadership styles (self-reported).

The subordinates responded to their **Preference for Leadership Style** (SP). The brief descriptions of the three styles—Authoritarian (F), Participative (P), and Nurturant-task (N)—were based on the above mentioned sources. Respondents evaluated the three through paired comparisons. The means for the preference of F, N, and P are 2.32, 3.33, and 3.35 and the *SDs* for the three are 1.54, 1.39, and 1.67, respectively.

The **Quality of Exchange** was measured through **Attention** (AT) and **Latitude** (LT) measures used by Dansereau, Alutto, and Yammarino (1984). The original measure of Attention contained 11 items, of which only five were chosen. Similarly, for Latitude, of the 11 original items, five were chosen. All such items that were thought to overlap directly or indirectly with the quality of interaction measure were left out. For the Attention measure the respondents evaluated on a five-point scale (*1 = Almost none; 5 = A great deal*) the *amount* of attention given to the subordinate by the leader. Taken only from the subordinate perspective, the *N* was 96. For latitude, the respondents evaluated on a four-point scale (*1 = no chance; 4 = certainly*) the *probability* of their leader giving the latitude. All the items of attention measure when subjected to a factor analysis clustered around one factor. Similarly, latitude also yielded one factor. Attention and latitude showed reliability coefficients of .91 and .90, means of 15.02 and 12.65, *SDs* of 5.56 and 3.92, and intercorrelation of .82. Although the correlation between the two is high, the two are treated as independent factors. **Quality of Interaction** was the third measure of quality of exchange, which is detailed in Chapter 3.

The **Influence Strategy** measures were evaluated only from the subordinate perspective. Therefore, the five factors that emerged in Study 1 were taken as they were. The relevant statistics of the strategies are given in Table 2.17.

Table 2.17

Scale Characteristics, Reliability Coefficients Alpha, and Intercorrelations of Influence Strategy Measures (Study 2)

	IS	I	PE	P	R
IS	.86				
I	.25	.85			
PE	.41	−.12	.87		
P	−.29	−.09	.17	.79	
R	−.58	−.07	−.20	.32	.86
M	18.07	14.65	12.85	21.85	20.19
SD	8.04	6.38	4.46	7.83	5.34
No. of items	6	5	6	3	4

Note: Diagonal entries indicate coefficients alpha; r (94) = .19 at $p < .05$; r (94) = .26 at $p < .01$; IS = Informal Support; I = Ingratiation; PE = Personalized Exchange; P = Persuasion; R = Reasoning.

The outcome variables of **Satisfaction** and **Commitment** were taken from Study 1. Extrinsic satisfaction, intrinsic satisfaction, and Commitment showed high reliabilities—.88, .84, and .88, respectively. Their means were 14.37, 15.96, and 38.41 and *SDs* were 4.07, 5.13, and 10.52, respectively. The intrinsic and extrinsic satisfaction subscales showed a correlation of .61.

The **Unit Effectiveness** (UE) scale (Mott, 1972), contained eight items. The subjects were asked to report their perceptions of their work unit on a five-point scale estimating the effectiveness. All the eight items were taken as constituting one single scale. A factor analysis yielded one factor and all the items loaded heavily, with factor loadings of .69, .69, .68, .67, .76, .74, .68, and .62. The scale showed an impressive reliability coefficient of .90, an M of 22.94, and a SD of 8.39.

Analysis

WABA

From methodological perspective, one of the key issues of our LMX/ VDL formulation is that of establishing the level at which leadership occurs, viz., group vs. dyad. To this, a Within-and-Between Analysis (WABA) given by Dansereau, Alutto and Yammarino (1984) is employed. Appendix III contains a sample analysis.

Other Traditional Analyses

Besides establishing the level of 'Quality of Interaction,' the present work also aimed at investigating some antecedents as well as consequences of the quality of interaction. The antecedents of the quality of exchange are hypothesized to be the interaction of some variables. Also the different dimensions of the quality of exchange are hypothesized to affect the outcome variables jointly (in interaction). Besides this, the independent effects of the quality of interaction dimensions too are hypothesized. Thus, we have two sets of analyses—one for investigating the interaction effects and the other for main effects.

Interaction Effects

As already mentioned, the interaction effects were hypothesized for all the antecedent conditions (Chapter 5) and for the outcome variables (Chapter 6).

The algebraic or statistical interaction has been largely analyzed with two techniques: analysis of variance (ANOVA) and multiple regression analysis. Different researchers have used different techniques (either ANOVA or multiple regression). 'This difference in analytic preference fits (well) with underlying assumptions about causes of behavior' (Schneider, 1983, p. 8). It needs to be mentioned, here, that the key construct of the present work—quality of interaction—is theoretically conceived of as a continuous variable (the leader's and the members' quality of interaction is supposed to vary continuously in a work-group). The division of a work-group (IN/OUT or High/Low LMX, etc.) only means that there are some distinct sub-groups in a work-group. "... scores on the negotiating latitude scale should not be grouped into artificial categories in that the underlying dimension is a continuous one" (Vecchio & Gobdel, 1984, p. 7). Because the multiple regression analysis preserves the continuous nature of the variables, it should be a preferred technique. In most cases, hence, multiple regression analysis was used to study the interactions. However, there were some interactions that involved two independent observations—that is, data both from the leaders and the members (e.g., the personal attributes of the two, leadership styles of the leader and the preference of the style by the members). Thus, to avoid common method variance, ANOVA was used. This is an unavoidable limitation of the analysis. Now, we discuss the two analyses very briefly.

Hierarchical Regression Analysis

As mentioned earlier, some of the interaction hypotheses were tested through hierarchical multiple regression analysis (Nie, Hull, Jenkins, Steinbrenner, & Bent 1975). For each interaction term, the variables were first converted to z-scores to give the scores equivalence, as they all roughly fall into the normal curve (i.e., $M = 0$; $SD = 1$). Finally the interaction term was taken as the product of these z-scores.

Instead of determining the incremental contribution of each variable by assuming it was added last, the hierarchical method requires the researcher to specify the order of inclusion. In the present study, the independent (or main) effects of the two variables were included at the first and second steps. Finally, at the third step, the interaction terms were included. The increment in R^2 at each step was taken as the component of variation. Thus, by taking the interaction terms at the third place, the confounding effects of the main effects were controlled. For an interaction hypothesis to be significant, the beta weights of the product term had to be significant. The significance of beta weights was tested through F-ratios. The formulae for computing Fs are slightly different from those employed in the standard multiple regression analysis (for details, see Nie, et al., 1975).

Significant interactions can further be analyzed graphically. Scores with ± one standard deviation from the means can be plotted (Hunt, Osborn, & Larson, 1975). The data in the means table are divided by the number of items. Further, in some cases, when one of the cells is empty, for these cells the means were predicted by the formula given by Winer (1971, pp. 487–490). If more than one cell is empty (had zero values), the interaction has to be left out. It needs to be mentioned here that the graphical representations show the direction of the interaction effects which is not shown by the beta weights. For the purpose of graphical representation, the data are grouped into qualitative categories (Low and High in the present study). Thus, it is possible that despite the beta weights being significant, the graphs of the same interaction might not look significant. This should be no cause of undue worry as the interaction is not a 'discontinuous qualitative variable that differentiates subgroups of individuals who are qualitatively different but is a continuous quantitative variable' (Zedeck, 1971, p. 305).

ANOVA

As mentioned earlier, some of the interaction hypotheses were tested through the application of analysis of variance (ANOVA). The F-ratios and their significance for the interaction term only were of interest.

All the interactions involved two variables. Each of these variables was divided into two categories—low and high—by splitting them at the median. Thus, a 2×2 ANOVA was used. Besides the F-ratios and their significance, means and n of each cell are also reported.

Further, just as in hierarchical regression, the interactions here are also shown graphically. The mean score in each cell is further divided by the number of items in the relevant scale. The details of ANOVA can be looked up in any standard book of statistics (e.g., Kirk, 1968; Winer, 1971).

Main Effects

Stepwise Regression

This method of stepwise regression—a variant of multiple regression—is a powerful technique of choosing a few best predictors from a set of independent variables.

In this method regression equations are created recursively. The best predictor (of a set of independent variables) comes at the first step, followed by the next best, and so on. This process continues till all the variables (that predict) are taken care of. This means that the first (at the first step) variable in the list is the best predictor. The next variable is a good predictor in conjunction with the first one, the third in conjunction with the first and second ones, and so on.

The significance of a particular predictor is a function of its beta weights. An *F*-ratio is calculated for these beta weights as a direct measure of their significance (for details, see Nie et al., 1975).

◄ Chapter 3 ►

Measuring the Dyadic Quality
of Interaction

An Overview

The present chapter reports the development of a scale to measure leader–member exchanges (LMX). It has been divided into four major parts.

The concept of 'LMX' is introduced in the first part of the chapter. The meaning is derived from the theoretical model presented in Chapter 1. The previous studies provide a useful background for deciphering the meaning. The LMX emerges as a multidimensional concept that has the potential to test the reciprocity in the dyad.

The different operationalizations of LMX are discussed in the next part. The first section in this part contains the basis on which the earliest measure (i.e., negotiating latitude) was developed. The next section discusses the key measures used in various studies. All the measures are unidimensional and few evaluate LMX from the leader perspective.

The third part deals with the development of a scale in line with the theoretical as well as the psychometric requirements. In the first section, the theoretical dimensions are stated. On the basis of these dimensions, the scale was developed. In the next section, the measurement aspects of the scale are taken up. First, the factor analysis results from both the leader and the member perspectives are reported. Second, some psychometric statistics, like reliability and validity, are provided. The level of analysis is, then, established. A test of ALS vs LMX status is conducted through WABA analysis. Finally, *mutuality* or *reciprocity* in a leader–member dyad is tested. The major findings and their implications are summarized in the last part of this chapter.

The Concept

The VDL or LMX theorization begins with the contention that the work-unit under a leader is not a single entity. The leader has different relationships with different members in the work-group. Also, the members have differential relationships with their leader and, consequently, they have different job-related attitudes and behaviors. Essentially, the focus is on a differential work-unit refuting the idea of homogeneity of a work-group.

Once the fact of a unit being differentiated is recognized, the next step is the identification of the aspects along which the leader–member interactions differ. Hence, the question is: what are the aspects of exchange (LMX) process along which the quality of exchange may vary within a work-group. To study the basis of unit differentiation, these aspects need to be delineated. Therefore, any operationalization of LMX should take into consideration these aspects of interaction or exchange.

Before we go on to see the various conceptualizations of LMX, a reconsideration of the theoretical bases is in order. It will give us the much needed insight into the aspects of interaction. This will also provide us the backdrop against which different operationalizations of LMX can be evaluated.

In the section on theoretical bases (see Chapter 1), we noted that the unit under a leader gets differentiated because some members collaborate with the leader on unstructured tasks and others do not. In the developmental framework, it is the end-result of role development by the members. In the process of developing their roles, the members through negotiations and exchanges imbibe collaboration on unstructured tasks in their roles. Where the collaboration is maximum, the jobs are done by the joint activities of the leader and the member. Hence, there is a total interdependence of the leader and the member to attain organizational objectives. In the work unit under a leader, there are different dyads with different levels of interdependence. Thus, the interdependence of the leader and the member is high for higher quality of exchanges and low for lower quality of exchanges. Dansereau et al. (1975) describe the possibility of a leader behaving in two different ways with the subordinates. These two behaviors were taken to develop the first measure of quality of exchange. It will be taken up in the next section.

If one were to see the basis of unit differentiation, one needs to identify the aspects of exchanges that lead to differing interdependence in different dyads. Graen and Scandura (1987) identify two dimensions of the exchanges that lead to interdependence between the leader and the member in a dyad. One aspect refers to the coupling of the leader and the member behaviors. This takes care of the reciprocal influence processes between the leader and the member. These are the actual negotiations between the two. This would involve the contributions of the members like increased effort and innovativeness, and members' inducements like increased influence in decision-making, and more latitude. The behaviors get interlocked because the leader's contributions are the members' inducements and the leader's inducements are the members' contributions. Thus, any operationalization of this coupling dimension would include these actual leader and member behaviors on the job.

The second dimension is relational or qualitative. We have already mentioned that once the role is routinized, some qualitative dimensions characterize the actual exchanges (Graen & Scandura, 1987). In a sense, these qualitative aspects are an outcome of the earlier exchange processes. To begin with, the different aspects of these two dimensions have to be identified to give a global measure of LMX. The need, hence, is to develop a multidimensional measure—a comprehensive measure of LMX.

Second, we have noted that the interaction or interdependence between the leader and the member is rooted in exchange processes. Therefore, any operationalization of the construct must incorporate the viewpoints of both the parties involved—the leader and the member. In other words, the measure should test the reciprocity or mutuality between the two parties (Dienesch & Liden, 1986). In addition, the measure should include such dimensions that at least have the potential to be evaluated both from the leader and the member perspectives. 'Mutuality implies that an exchange must develop along dimensions to which both parties can contribute' (ibid., p. 624). These are the requirements, hence, that are to be met with while operationalizing the construct of LMX.

LMX Operationalizations: A Review

The Background

In the formulation of the VDL theory, Dansereau et al. (1975) identified the possibility of a leader indulging in two different kinds of behaviors with the subordinates. For this, they took a clue from Jacob's (1970) distinction between 'leadership' and 'supervision' as two techniques.

> Employing the *supervision* technique, the nature of the vertical exchange is such that a superior relies almost exclusively upon the formal employment contract in his exchanges with the member....In contrast, employing the technique of *leadership*, the nature of the vertical exchange is such that the superior cannot rely exclusively upon the employment contract. Instead, he must seek a different basis for influencing the behavior of a member. This alternative basis of influence is anchored in the interpersonal exchange relationship between a superior and a member (Dansereau et al., 1975, p. 49, emphases added).

> The indulgence of one leader in these different behaviors results in a differentiated unit. In the role development framework, we noticed that the negotiations on role took place only with those members who collaborated on unstructured tasks. Alternatively, the amount of negotiation on the roles defines the quality of exchanges between the leader and the member as greater latitude means greater use of leadership and lesser use of supervision (Dansereau et al. 1975).

The Operationalizations

In the discovery study, Dansereau et al. (1975) conceptualized LMX in terms of the negotiating latitude, which was defined as 'the extent to which a superior is willing to consider requests from a member concerning role development' (ibid., p. 51). This was a longitudinal study, and the latitude given to the members at the initial stage was the predictor of different outcomes at later stages. Negotiating latitude was operationalized in terms of two items. In that study factors such as the leader support and attention were treated as outcomes. Dienesch and Liden (1986) criticize the above study because the variables that are treated as outcomes are, according to them, alternate measures of LMX. But since the study is longitudinal, it treats negotiating latitude as the antecedent of the exchanges that take place at a later stage. We will come back to this a little later. Right now, let us evaluate the other measures used in previous studies to assess LMX.

Following the initial two-item operationalization (Dansereau et al., 1975), there have been many formulations and reformulations of the LMX measure. Table 3.1 lists various studies and the measures of LMX used in them.

Even a cursory look at Table 3.1 shows that the construct of LMX has seen various formulations in its short life span. Before we discuss the relatively stable measures (that have been used in at least two studies), let us first concentrate on the measures used in one study only.

In the Rosse and Kraut (1983) study, the traditional measure was not used, as the data were a part of the larger study. The items were not designed to test the VDL model. All the same, Rosse and Kraut picked up four items that could be considered to tap members' reported negotiating latitude (MNL). Of these, two items were concerned with the management but were rated by the 14 expert judges as reflecting the negotiating latitude given by the manager to the subordinate. Similarly, the 14 judges identified four items that could tap the leader's reported negotiating latitude (LNL), and construct validity was obtained by correlating these measures of negotiating latitude with other outcomes like job latitude and open and honest communications (Rosse & Kraut, 1983). These are the variables that were also taken as outcomes in the Dansereau et al. (1975) study. These measures (LNL and MNL) are given a detailed treatment in the study to justify their inclusion in the measures of LMX.

Kim and Organ (1982), in their study, used a scale which they called the 'Noncontractual Social Exchange' scale. They developed

Table 3.1
Quality of Exchange Measures Used in Empirical Studies

Study	Measure
Dansereau, Graen, & Haga (1975)	NL (2 items)
Graen & Cashman (1975)	NL (4 items)
Cashman, Dansereau, Graen, & Haga (1976)	NL (2 items)
Graen, Cashman, Ginsburgh, & Schiemann (1977)	NL (4 items)
Graen & Ginsburgh (1977)	NL (2 items)
Graen & Schiemann (1978)	NL (4 items)
Schriesheim (1979)	LBDQ-XII
Katerberg & Hom (1981)	LBDQ
Graen, Novak, & Sommerkamp (1982)	LMX (7 items)
Graen, Liden, & Hoel (1982)	LMX (5 items)
Kim & Organ (1982)	NSE*
Vecchio (1982)	LPC
Rosse & Kraut (1983)	MNL* (4 items) and LNL* (4 items)
Vecchio & Gobdel (1984)	NL (4 items)
Seers & Graen (1984)	NL (4 items)
Scandura & Graen (1984)	LMX (7 items)
Wakabayashi & Graen (1984)	LMX (12 items)
Ferris (1985)	LMX (5 items)
Snyder & Bruning (1985)	NL (4 items)
Duchon, Green, & Taber (1986)	LMX (5 items)
Scandura, Graen, & Novak (1986)	LMX (7 items)
Wakabayashi, Graen, Graen, & Graen (1988)	LMX (12 items)
Kozlowski & Doherty (1989)	LMX (7 items) and IE (8 items)
Schrieshiem, Neider, Scandura, & Tepper (1992)	LMX (6 items)

Note: * Scales used in one study only. Abbreviations: NL = Negotiating Latitude; LBDQ = Leader Behavior Description Questionnaire; LMX = Leader–Member Exchange; NSE = Non-contractual Social Exchange; LPC = Least Preferred Coworker; LNL = Leaders' Negotiating Latitude; MNL = Members' Negotiating Latitude; IE = Information Exchange.

the scale with an assumption that the exchanges between the leader and the member need to be evaluated on a continuous scale. They took the concept of 'exchanges' between a leader and a member. They also argued that it is the leader who initiates a typical exchange process. Consequently, their scale measured the noncontractual social exchange from the *leader's perspective*. Their scale contained 15 items (from a pool of 20 items) and included items such as, 'I would give him personal favors,' 'I would initiate discussion with him on his personal problems to help him.' The leader evaluated each member in terms of these items. The leader's evaluation of the subordinates in terms of these items has its own problems that are discussed later.

Kozlowski and Doherty (1989) used an information exchange (IE) scale in addition to a seven-item version of the LMX scale. For the IE scale, they began with 13 items but the final scale, based on factor analysis, retained only eight items. The items included those few aspects that differentiated between the IN and OUT group statuses. It involved giving information both upwards and downwards. The scale was used only from the subordinate perspective; hence, the member evaluated how much information or 'scoop' the leader gave him or her, and also how much information (scoop) he or she gave to the leader. The emphasis was on information exchange both in terms of advice on the job and personal matters. It also included items directly asking the member's status in the IN- or the OUT-Group. The scale showed a high correlation with the seven-item LMX version ($r = .73$, $N = 165$, $p < .01$), thereby providing an evidence of concurrent validity that both the scales were measuring almost the same construct. But, Kozlowski and Doherty (1989) concluded: 'The parallelism between the LMX measure and the IE measure was noteworthy, with the LMX measure being consistenly superior' (ibid., p. 550). This might be because the IE scale measured only one aspect of leader–member exchanges (i.e., the information exchange). As a result, it gave a narrow and peripheral conceptualization of the construct.

Next, we take up all those measures that have been used in more than one study. An inspection of Table 3.1 shows that there have been various operationalizations of the construct. But, once we look at each of the scales, we find that there is a lot of overlap between the items. The original two items of the negotiating latitude scale (Dansereau et al., 1975) have been retained in all the subsequent formulations. So, essentially, the later formulations are only extensions of the original scale. Table 3.2 presents a pool of all the items used in the four LMX scales: two-item negotiating latitude, four-item negotiating latitude, five-item LMX, and seven-item LMX. The 12-item vertical exchange scale will be taken up separately. Table 3.3 shows the actual composition of these different versions.

Table 3.2

Pool of Items Used in Different LMX Measures

(1) How flexible do you believe your supervisor is about evolving change in your job?

(2) Regardless of how much formal organizational authority your supervisor has built into his position, what are the chances that he would be personally inclined to use his power to help you solve problems in your work?

(3) To what extent can you count on your supervisor to 'bail you out' at his expense when you really need him?

(4) How often do you take your suggestions regarding your work to your supervisor?

(5) How would you characterize your working relationship with your supervisor?

(6) Do you usually feel that you know where you stand ... do you usually know how satisfied your immediate superior is with what you do?

(7) How well do you feel that your immediate supervisor understands your problems and needs?

(8) How well do you feel that your immediate supervisor recognizes your potential?

(9) I have enough confidence in my supervisor that I would defend and justify his or her decisions if he or she were not present to do so.

Thus far, we have traced a brief history of the items of negotiating latitude. The two items, originally coined in the Dansereau et al. study, have been included in all the versions of the LMX measure. We have mentioned earlier that the Dansereau et al. (1975) study was a longitudinal study, and measuring latitude at an earlier stage of role development was the right choice. In other cases, one begins with the assumption that the exchanges are relatively stable and enters the units at a time when the relationships in dyads have stabilized. For a cross-sectional study at this stage, it is advisable to include relational dimensions, as they are more salient at this stage, and instead of talking only about the latitude given, one can also talk of the contribution of the two parties on the jobs.

The other versions of the LMX measure include elements of subordinate competence, trust, satisfaction of the leader with the member, leader support, etc. This clearly shows that there has always been a felt need to extend the measure but the attempt has always left something desired. The need, hence, is to develop a multidimensional measure that incorporates the different aspects of interaction.

Table 3.3
Constitution of LMX Measures

The Measures	No. of Items	Items Used*
Negotiating Latitude	2	1,2
Negotiating Latitude	4	1,2,3,4
LMX	5	1,2,3,4,5
LMX	7	1,2,5,6,7,8,9

Note: *The numbers are the corresponding items in Table 3.2; LMX = Leader–Member Exchange.

And, now a word about the 12-item vertical exchange or LMX scale used in a longitudinal study by Wakabayashi and his associates. A longitudinal observation was started in Japan in the early 1970s to evaluate the career progress of the new entrants. The researchers administered the vertical exchange scale to these new members to evaluate their standing with respect to the leader. Whenever these members joined new leaders, the vertical exchange was measured. The exchange was measured by a 12-item (English-language) scale, which is reported in the seven-year (Wakabayashi & Graen, 1984) and the 13-year (Wakabayashi et al., 1988) follow-up studies. The 12 items had elements of accessibility, flexibility, and willingness of the supervisor to use his authority and help the subordinate. It also assesses the freedom or the latitude the subordinate had in designing his role and off-the-job social interactions. This study also evaluates the leader–member exchanges at the initial stages and hence the inclusion of flexibility, superior expectations, support, etc. is justified.

It also needs to be pointed out that, with the exception of a few studies (e.g., Wakabayashi & Graen, 1984; Wakabayashi et al., 1988), studies have not incorporated the leader's evaluation of LMX. Kim and Organ (1982), on the other extreme, have taken only the leader's evaluation of noncontractual exchange. Duchon et al. (1986) have used the sociometric ratings of the leaders for the individual members as a corroborative evidence. Graen and Scandura (1987) point out that sometimes the supervisors may give a socially desirable response of treating all their subordinates alike. But, as was pointed out earlier, the dyadic interactions need to be evaluated by both the parties involved. The problem of 'social desirability' can be overcome if one party evaluates the contribution(s) of the other party. Thus, asking a leader how much a particular member works or contributes on jobs is liable to get much more objective responses. The member can also be asked the same question for the leader.

It may be concluded that the measures developed so far fail to tap the different aspects of the interaction. Second, they also generally fail to incorporate the evaluations of *both* the parties involved.

Development of the Scale*

The Background

One of the main objectives of the present study is to develop a scale that is comprehensive and involves different aspects of interaction. In other words, a multidimensional scale is envisaged to be developed. Second, the choice of the dimensions needs to be dealt with, with utmost care. Only those dimensions need be taken that can be evaluated *both* by the leader and the member.

Our selection of the dimensions fell on the *three* dimensions given by Dienesch and Liden (1986). Dinesch and Liden propose an employment of the following three dimensions to meet the above mentioned two criteria:

(a) *Perceived contribution* to the exchange—perception of the amount, direction, and quality of work-oriented activity each member puts forth toward the mutual goals (explicit or implicit) of the dyad; (b) *Loyalty*—the expression of public support for the goals and the personal character of the other member of the LMX dyad (emphasis is on public support/symbolic actions for the benefit of third parties—not suppression of dissent or debate within the leader–member relationship; the good team player approach); (c) *Affect*—the mutual affection the members of the dyad have for each other based primarily on interpersonal attraction rather than work or professional values (ibid., p. 625, emphases added).

* A part of this section has been published earlier (Bhal & Ansari, 1996).

These dimensions take care of the quality of interaction on-the-job (perceived contribution and loyalty) and off-the-job (affect). Graen and Scandura (1987) do talk of relational aspects but these aspects are not independent of work. They include relational dimensions on the work itself. Hence, the actual behavioral (coupling) dimension and qualitative dimension may not really be two independent dimensions. Thus, we incorporate both the aspects *but* the relational dimension becomes essentially affective in nature. It may be argued that although the two dimensions are presumed to be separate, the elements of the two are intercorrelated. As Homans (1951) points out 'if the interactions between the members of a group are frequent in the external (task) system, sentiments of liking will grow up between them' (ibid., p. 112).

Once the scale has been developed, the second objective is to evaluate the levels at which the measure is to be understood. First, it aims to identify whether the leader shows differences in evaluating different subordinates (leader perspective). Second, it aims to see whether the different members in a unit evaluate their leader differently (member perspective).

Finally, it is proposed to examine whether the leader and the member in a dyad show reciprocity. In other words, the study aims to see whether there is a similarity of perception within a dyad.

Measurement

Preliminaries

A number of items were identified in the above mentioned three dimensions. After a pilot study, the items were refined and reworded by weeding out the weak items, modifying the ambiguous ones, and so on. The questionnaire, in Study 1, contained 24 items (one item reverse scored). Of these 24, nine items were composed of perceived contribution, seven of loyalty, and eight of affect dimensions (Appendix I). The scale was named 'Quality of Interaction' (QI) scale. The use of the term 'exchange' was deliberately avoided, as it was not the exchanges (in terms of behavioral inducements and contributions) that were being evaluated. Of course, the three dimensions taken, if evaluated from both the perspectives, are explained and understood in an exchange framework.

But, all the studies might not aim to evaluate these dimensions from both the perspectives; they could be interested in evaluating either perspective (e.g., for predicting outcomes for the members). In Study 1, a total of 304 responses were obtained on this section of the questionnaire—152 responses were the leader's evaluations of the members and 152 were those of the members' for the leaders. Thus, there were 152 dyads. The respondents were asked to evaluate (on a seven-point scale, *1 = not at all*; *7 = very much*) the *degree* to which each item was true for the interaction between him or her and the other person (the leader's or the member's name, with whom the interaction was evaluated, was mentioned).

In Study 2, only those items and dimensions of the QI Scale were taken that emerged after the factor analysis of the scale in Study 1. The results of factor analysis will be discussed in the following section. In Study 2, only the members (*N* = 96) evaluated the interaction with their leaders. The instructions were the same as in Study 1. These 96 members belonged to 26 work-groups, with mostly four but sometimes three members in a group.

Empirical Test of the QI Scale

Factor Analysis Results and Discussion

All the 24 items in Study 1 were subjected to a varimax rotated factor analysis, as a partial test of the construct validity. First, the data were pooled from both the perspectives—leader and member (*N* = 304)—to investigate their common factor structure.

The analysis yielded two neat factors containing 10 items. Only those factors were included that had a eigenvalue around 1. Items in a factor were retained only when the factor loadings were above .50 and cross-loadings generally below .30. When the loadings of an item on the factor were very high, the criterion of cross-loadings was relaxed a little, and the item was allowed to stay on the factor. The factor loadings obtained are given in Table 3.4. The same analysis was repeated for the members' evaluations (*N* = 152). The results constrained to the same two dimensions. These factor loadings are also provided in Table 3.4. In both the cases (i.e., the combined data and the member perspective), the two factors explained all the variances. In both of them, the first factor (i.e., perceived contribution) explained around 85 per cent of the variance. The data for the leader's perspective ($N = 152$) were also subjected to a factor analysis. Although the results for the leader's perspective yielded three factors, *none* of the items in the second factor met the requirement of cross-loadings below or around .30. *All* the items that loaded heavily on the second factor had high cross-loadings on factor 1 (usually the magnitude being .40 and above). Therefore, only factor 1 and factor 3 were included. In this case, the two factors together explained a total of 86.3 percent of the variance. For these factor loadings also, see Table 3.4. Table 3.5 shows the inter-item and item-test correlations.

The first factor, in all the three factor analyses, contained five items. All these items corresponded to the contribution on the job and, hence, the factor was called, *Perceived Contribution* (PC). The contribution was evaluated in terms of responsibility taken, efficiency, usefulness (relevance), amount of effort, and initiativeness. For both the leader and the member perspectives (and also the combined data), this was the first and the most powerful factor. This reveals the centrality of 'contribution' on the job *both* from the leader and the member perspectives.

The second factor included five items of mutual liking, and was called, *Affect* (AF). The items included discussing and seeking advice on personal problems, amount of interaction off-the-job, taking help in personal matters, and so on. A closer scrutiny of Table 3.5 shows that the item on interaction off-the-job (item 7) shows a relatively weaker (though acceptable) item-test correlation. This is probably because interaction off-the-job is a function of some other variables, besides affect, like home location, religious affiliations, etc. (Crouch & Yetton, 1988). For both the leaders and the members, affect was the second factor that explained much less variance than the first factor.

The emergence of two factors in the same order for both the leaders and the members confirms that the dimensions chosen have the potential to be evaluated by both—the leader and the member—without any biases. This also provides an evidence for the stability of factor structures for the subscales, as for the two sets of respondents (the leader and the member) identical factors emerged. The two factors were only moderately intercorrelated ($r = .50$ for the combined data), thereby showing a great deal of independence.

Table 3.4
Factor Loadings Obtained—Quality of Interaction Scale (Study 1)

	Combined		Member		Leader	
Items	F1	F2	F1	F2	F1	F2
4. How much responsibility does he/ she take for the jobs that are to be done together by you and him/ her?	81	29	83	24	74	29
15. How much is his/her contribution to the quantity of solutions on the jobs that are to be done together by you and him/her?	82	20	82	22	73	14
17. How efficient is his/her contribution on the jobs for which the two of you work together?	82	30	82	27	70	30
21. How useful is his/her effort on the jobs that are to be done together by you and him/her?	84	29	83	30	78	24
24. How much initiative does he/she take in solving the problems that are to be done together by you and him/her?	80	32	76	34	71	26
7. How much do you interact with each other off-the- job?	32	61	34	56	16	68
13. How much do you help each other in personal matters?	14	88	10	87	20	88
16. How much advice do you seek from each other on personal problems?	21	88	18	90	23	85
19. How much do you discuss your personal matters with each other?	18	90	15	90	15	90
23. How much importance do you attach to each other's advice on personal matters?	31	76	32	74	24	76
Eigenvalue	14.00	2.38	13.73	2.44	14.38	.84
Percentage of Variance	85.50	14.50	84.90	15.10	81.50	4.80

Note: F1 = Perceived contribution; F2 = Affect; Decimal points in factor loadings have been omitted.

Table 3.5

Descriptive Statistics, Inter-item Correlations, and Item-total Correlations of the Quality of Interaction Scale (Study 1)

Items*	4	15	17	21	24	7	13	16	19	23
4	–									
15	.72	–								
17	.75	.82	–							
21	.77	.78	.81	–						
24	.75	.75	.78	.80	–					
7	.40	.38	.46	.43	.43	–				
13	.37	.29	.38	.38	.40	.58	–			
16	.40	.37	.45	.42	.46	.58	.82	–		
19	.40	.32	.42	.40	.45	.61	.83	.88	–	
23	.47	.35	.45	.48	.50	.59	.70	.69	.72	–
M	5.13	4.92	4.94	5.01	4.90	3.44	3.40	3.07	3.03	3.81
SD	1.46	1.36	1.34	1.36	1.45	1.75	1.61	1.47	4.07	1.64
Item-Test r	.81	.84	.87	.87	.85	.65	.84	.85	.87	.76

Note: *For the description of the items, refer to Table 3.4; N = 304.

Of the three hypothesized factors (perceived contribution, loyalty, and affect), only two emerged. *Loyalty* did not emerge at all probably because both the parties involved (i.e., the leader and the member) evaluate the relationship at the dyadic level and the interaction with the other members of the group is not considered important. But the two dimensions that emerge cover the two broad areas—the behavioral contribution on the job and the affective reactions of the two.

The means, SDs, and coefficients alpha of the QI factors can be looked up in Table 3.6.

Psychometric Properties

The reliabilities (Cronbach's coefficents alpha) of the scales in both the studies are reported in Table 3.6. It is clearly evident that the scales have very impressive reliability coefficients, ranging between .91 and .95.

To test the concurrent validity of the scales, a five-item LMX measure was included in Study 1. The two factors—perceived contribution and affect—correlated highly with the LMX measure. The correlations are given in Table 3.7. Perceived contribution showed a higher correlation than affect with the five-item LMX scale. This

Table 3.6
Descriptive Statistics and Coefficients Alpha of the QI Scales

	Sample	Subscale	Mean	SD	Alpha
	COM (N = 304)	PC	24.92	6.31	.94
		AF	16.75	6.90	.92
STUDY 1	L (N = 152)	PC	24.57	6.28	.95
		AF	16.10	6.49	.93
	M (N = 152)	PC	25.26	6.35	.93
		AF	17.41	7.25	.91
STUDY 2	M (N = 96)	PC	22.08	7.34	.93
		AF	17.16	7.62	.92

Note: COM = Combined data; L = Leader perspective; M = Member perspective; PC = Perceived Contribution; AF = Affect; Each subscale consisted of five items.

is probably because the LMX scale measures the behaviors on the job very much like the perceived contribution. In Study 2, the Attention and Latitude measures were used to reassess the concurrent validity. The correlations of newly developed measures (perceived contribution and affect) with attention and latitude (Table 3.7) were quite high. This too should be considered a partial evidence of external validity.

So far, we have seen the development of a scale which has two dimensions, with strong reliabilities and some evidence of external validity. This is a scale that takes care of both the leader and the member perspectives. Next, we go on to see whether the scale shows unit differentiation or not. Finally, we test the aspect of mutuality in a leader–member dyad.

Establishment of the Level

Within- and Between-Person and Work-Group

As has been pointed out, the VDL/LMX approach focuses on the individual members, not the work-group. Although there are

Table 3.7

Relationships of Perceived Contribution (PC) and Affect (AF) with Other Measures of Quality of Exchange (Member Perspective)

	PC	AF
Study 1[a]		
LMX	.77	.52
Study 2[b]		
AT	.81	.72
LT	.68	.69

Note: [a] $N = 152$; [b] $N = 96$; AT = Attention; LT = Latitude; LMX = Leader–Member Exchange.

certain aspects of leadership that could be applicable to the work-group as a whole, the measures developed on the basis of exchange model should show within-group variance. Since the quality of interaction measures have been developed in this framework, they are expected to reveal these variations.

The analysis is conducted from two perspectives—the leader and the member. From the leader perspective, the objective is to see whether the leader differentiates between different members in terms of their contribution on-the-job and his or her affect for them. If he or she does, the within person (i.e., the leader) variance should be more and if the individual leaders differ, the between-variance should be more. If neither exists, a reject condition is established. For this purpose, a very small sample was available. Only the leaders in Synthetics Limited (Study 1) evaluated around four members each. In all the other organizations, each leader evaluated only two members. Two is too small a number to study within-group variance. Hence, only the leaders in the organization mentioned above were put through this analysis. Eleven leaders evaluated 40 members ($N = 40$). The results of WABA analysis for this sample are presented in Table 3.8. The analysis shows that within-*eta* correlations are higher than between-*eta* correlations for both—perceived contribution and affect. Although perceived contribution and affect show significant E-ratios, F-ratios are not significant for either. This is probably because F-ratios are sensitive to sample size which is too small here ($N = 40$). The findings imply that the leader evaluates the different members in the work-group differently in terms of their contribution on the job and his or her affect for them, thereby establishing a person-part level. A closer examination of the *E*-ratios for perceived contribution and affect shows that whereas the person- part level is established strongly for perceived contribution, it is weakly established for the affect dimension. There is a probability that the leaders are more objective and factual in evaluating different members' contribution on the job. But, while reporting their feelings or affect for the members, they become somewhat defensive.

Table 3.8
WABA: Within-and-Between Person (Leader) Analysis (Study 1)

	PC	AF
eta between (10)	.44	.58
eta within (29)	.90	.81
E-Ratio	.49	.72
F-Ratio	.70	1.50
Inferences		
WHOLES		
15° E ≥ 1.30		
30° E ≥ 1.73		
.05 F ≥ 2.18		
.01 F ≥ 3.00		
PARTS		
15° E ≤ .77	#	#
30° E ≤ .58	#	
.05 F ≤ .37		
.01 F ≤ .23		
REJECT		
15° (all others)		
30° (all others)	#	
.05 (all others)	#	#
.01 (all others)	#	#

Note: $N = 40$; # shows the location of data (level); numbers in parantheses are the degrees of freedom.

From the members' perspective also, a similar analysis was done. The reference now is made to the work-group. The aim is to evaluate whether members in a work-group evaluate their leader differently in terms of leader's contribution on the job and their affect for the leader. For this purpose again, sufficiently larger work-group is needed (around four). Hence, we analyze the data from Study 2 where 96 members belonging to 26 work-groups responded to the questionnaire.

A WABA analysis for the work-group level would be a direct test of the Average (ALS) *vs* the VDL models. The establishment of a whole work-group level would be the evidence of an average nature of leadership, whereas a work-group parts level would be the evidence of a non-average nature of leadership.

The results indicate that, broadly, both perceived contribution and affect show an evidence for a differentiated unit (see Table 3.9). Thus, the results for the member prespective are similar to those of the leader perspective. For perceived contribution, within-*eta* correlation is much higher than the between-*eta* correlation.

Table 3.9
WABA: Within-and-Between Work-Group (Member) Analysis (Study 2)

	PC	AF
eta between (26)	.43	.53
eta within (69)	.90	.85
E-Ratio	.48	.62
F-Ratio	.61	1.02
Inferences		
WHOLES		
15° E ≥ 1.30		
30° E ≥ 1.73		
.05 F ≥ 2.18		
.01 F ≥ 3.00		
PARTS		
15° E ≤ 0.77	#	#
30° E ≤ 0.58	#	
.05 F ≤ 0.37		
.01 F ≤ 0.23		
REJECT		
15° (all others)		
30° (all others)	#	
.05 (all others)	#	#
.01 (all others)	#	#

Note: $N = 96$; # shows the location of data (level); numbers in parantheses are the degrees of freedom.

Although the results for affect are also similar, the difference is not strong enough. This could be so because affective components of the interaction are not strong enough (see factor analysis results).

All the same, from the subordinate perspective, generally, there is an evidence of LMX/VDL model of leadership. In other words, the dimensions of perceived contribution and affect provide support to the LMX model from the leader as well as the member perspectives.

Within- and-Between Dyad Analysis

Now, we shift our attention to the dyad containing a leader and a member. Both the leaders and the members evaluate each other on the two dimensions of perceived contribution and affect. The objective is to see whether the leader and the member in a dyad evaluate each other similarly on these two dimensions. For this purpose, a within- and between-dyad analysis was performed. The 152 leader–member dyads in Study 1 were the input to this case. In other words, this is a test of 'reciprocity' or 'mutuality' of perception.

The analysis shows that between-*eta* correlations for both the dimensions were significantly higher than the within-*eta* correlations (see Table 3.10). This evidence is obviously for a whole dyad level.

The results imply that there is a *mutuality* of perception between the leader and the member. Thus, if the leader feels that the member's contribution is high on the jobs, the member also feels the same for the leader. Conversely speaking, if the leader feels that the member's contribution is low on the job the member also perceives the same for the leader. This finding is directly in tune with collaboration structure. For the high quality dyad, there is a lot of interaction between the two parties, as the two are interdependent for the achievement of organizational goals. For the lower quality dyad, the interaction is less as the collaboration and interdependence are minimal. Consequently, both the parties perceive less contribution on the job for each other.

On the dimension of affect also, the leader and the member in a dyad displayed mutuality. Blau (1964) points out that the balance of mutuality is crucial for the relationship to grow and develop. In the initial stages of interaction, there are chances of a mismatch between the affective reactions because the parties are still in an

Table 3.10

WABA: *Within-and-Between Dyad Analysis (Study 1)*

	PC	A
eta between (151)	.92	.86
eta within (152)	.40	.59
E-Ratio	2.30	1.69
F-Ratio 5.34 2.86		
Inferences		
WHOLES		
15° E ≥ 1.30	#	#
30° E ≥ 1.73	#	
.05 F ≥ 1.31	#	#
.01 F ≥ 1.47	#	#
PARTS		
15° E ≤ 0.77		
30° E ≤ 0.58		
.05 F ≤ 0.76		
.01 F ≤ 0.68		
REJECT		
15° E (all others)		
30° E (all others)	#	
.05 F (all others)		
.01 F (all others)		

Note: N = 304; # shows the location of data (level); numbers in parantheses are the degrees of freedom.

evaluative state. The affective reactions of the two parties become mutual once the relationship is established, as is the case in our sample.

Summary

The VDL or the LMX model conceives of a work-unit under a leader as composed of leader–member dyads. The dyads in a unit differ in terms of the interdependence of the two parties for the achievement of organizational ends. At the most positive extreme, the two parties—the leader and the member—are totally dependent on each other; at the most negative end, there is very little interdependence. Thus, any measure of LMX must take into consideration the different aspects of this interdependence. Also, since one is focusing on the dyad, LMX must test the reciprocity of perception in the dyad. This would mean evaluating LMX from both the leader and the member perspectives.

A review of literature indicates that the LMX measure has been constantly in transition. Besides this, most measures are unidimensional and do not attempt to test reciprocity, although in a few studies, LMX has been measured from the leader perspective.

An attempt is made to develop a scale that would overcome the limitations of the earlier measures. Theoretically, three dimensions are identified that can be tested both from the leader and the member perspectives. When the scale, based on these dimensions, is subjected to a factor analysis, just two emerge. The two factors are the perceived contribution of the other party in the dyad and the mutual affection between the two of them. The same two dimensions emerge from both the leader and the member perspectives. Perceived contribution seems to be stronger than affect from both the perspectives.

Next, we pose the question: do the elements of perceived contribution and affect occur at a group level, or are they different for different members? The leader does evaluate different members differently on both the aspects. The different members also evaluate their leaders differently on the above mentioned two dimensions. This points towards a differentiated unit. This also means that the different members will have different job related attitudes and behaviors. This contention is examined in Chapter 5.

Finally, the analysis revealed a *mutuality* in the leader's and the member's evaluations of each other. This means that some consequent leader activities and behaviors can be predicted by the leader's evaluation of the member's perceived contribution and the affection between the two.

◄ Chapter 4 ►

Compatibility as a Determinant of Dyadic Interactions

An Overview

In the last chapter, we provided evidence for the fact that the leaders' interaction with their subordinates varies in a work-group along the dimensions of perceived contribution and affect. The next logical step is to identify the variables that are instrumental in causing differentiation of the unit in terms of dyadic quality of interaction. It is, hence, a search for the variables which to some extent may determine the quality of interaction. This chapter is an attempt in this direction. One point needs to be noted at the outset: since we are focusing on *interaction* between the leader and the subordinates, the antecedents too are seen as the interaction of variables related to the two of them, i.e., the leader and the member. It is a typical person–environment interaction where in some cases, one person of the dyad may provide the environment for another person. Investigations are broadly aimed at ascertaining whether the dyadic interactions are a function of (*i*) leaders' and members' general predispositions towards work like their social needs; (*ii*) preferred leadership orientations; or (*iii*) the backdrop, i.e., organizational climate.

The Background

Prior to discussing the relevant variables employed in the present investigations, the general nature of the hypotheses needs to be mentioned. Since our focus is on the quality of interaction, its determinants are also seen as an interaction of variables related to the leaders and the members. Interactional psychology has emerged as an answer to the person–situation interaction controversy (Bowers, 1973). Hence, the organization-related phenomena like leadership, socialization, etc. are understood in terms of person by environment interaction.

In the context of leadership, the recent emphasis on contingency approaches seems to be a manifestation of interactional psychology. Whereas some theorists (e.g., Ansari, 1990; Hersey & Blanchard, 1982; J.B.P. Sinha, 1980; Vroom & Yetton, 1973) focus on the *interaction* between leadership behavior and situations, others (e.g., Fiedler, 1973) focus on the trait (orientation) by situation *interaction*. These macro-level average theories of leadership study the interactions to determine the effectiveness of a leader.

In the micro-level framework of leadership, the focus is on the dyad—a dyad consisting of a leader and a member. The basis of unit differentiation (i.e., quality of interaction) is the key variable, which needs to be understood in interactional terms, for which the relevant personal and situational variables need to be identified. Also, since the construct is based on the interaction between the leader and the member, an interaction of the variables related to the two of them is likely to yield fruitful insights.

Personal Orientations

The Background

We have stressed in Chapter 1 the need to study the *compatibility* of the personal orientations of the leader and the member (Graen and Cashman, 1975). We also mentioned that the leader evaluates the motivations/needs of the members which, to a large extent, determines their quality of exchange. The leader evaluates the member in the framework of his or her own motivations/needs. Hence, we take the need orientations of the two as a starting point.

Since the organization is conceived of as a collection of interacting and interdependent individuals, the individual needs and motives (in the context of work situation) cannot be isolated from more direct organizational phenomena. We begin with an understanding of the term 'need' before examining its relevance to the organizational framework. According to Murray (1938), it may be seen as a force within the individual which organizes the individual's perceptual and other processes, on the one hand, and on the other may get provoked by the external environment.

Murray has identified a list of twenty needs. The list includes the needs for abasement, achievement, affiliation, aggression, autonomy, counteraction, defendance, deference, dominance, exhibition, harm avoidance, infavoidance, nurturance, order, play, rejection, sentinence, sex, succorance, and understanding. Of these 20 needs, four—needs for power, achievement, affiliation, and autonomy—have been found to be of considerable interest to work behavior (Atkinson, 1964; McClelland, Atkinson, Clark, & Lowell, 1953). Thus, the present work examines these four needs, which are described below.

Need for Achievement (n Ach)

It is defined as the competitive behavior aimed towards excellence (McClelland et al., 1953). People high on *n* Ach (*i*) assume personal responsibility for completing the task, (*ii*) set moderately challenging goals and take calculated risks—that is, they set challenging *but* realistic goals, (*iii*) they look for concrete feedback on task performance, and (*iv*) have a complete involvement in the task and its completion. In contrast, those who are low on *n* Ach prefer jobs that are done jointly by a number of people and involve low risks.

Need for Power (n Pow)

It is a desire to influence people and control the environment around self. This they do by vocally presenting their ideas, views, and opinions and by taking leadership positions in the group. They are usually fluent, vocal, and often seen as forceful and outspoken (Litwin & Stringer 1968).

Need for Autonomy (n Aut)

It is defined as 'a desire for independence and for freedom from any kinds of constraints' (Steers & Porter, 1987, p. 62). People with high n Aut (i) like to work independently on jobs, (ii) be in command of their work speed, and (iii) do not like the interference of rules and regulations on their jobs (Birsch & Veroff, 1966).

Need for Affiliation (n Aff)

It is defined as 'attraction to another organism in order to feel reassured from the other that the self is acceptable' (Birsch & Veroff, 1966, p. 65). People with high n Aff are characterized by a desire to get other people's assurances and approval which they try to get by conforming to their wishes and showing a genuine interest in their feelings.

These four needs are taken as relatively fixed personality orientations. Universalists, while theorizing leadership, would place them in the category of traits. Most of the studies of need orientations have concentrated on delineating their importance in predicting leadership effectiveness.

Need for Achievement is considered an important need for the leaders to be effective (McClelland, 1961; McClelland & Winter, 1969), as it has been shown to predict managerial success reliably (Ansari et al., 1982), i.e., there exists a positive relationship between rate of career progression and n Ach(e.g., Meyer & Walker, 1961). However, Steers and Porter (1987) note that since high n Ach managers are more concerned about gaining independence on and responsibility for the job, they are less likely to be effective when they have to manage people.

Need for power is a much studied value orientation in the context of leadership in organizations. Zaleznik (1970) is of the opinion that organizations regardless of their nature are political entities and they operate by distributing authority and setting the stage for the exercise of power. Consequently, 'power is said to be institutionalized in leadership roles or *offices*' (Winter & Stewart, 1978, p. 400, emphases in original). Thus, there are required environmental presses in the role of the leader for n Pow to be satisfied. The next question obviously relates to effectiveness. Although Shaw and Harkey (1976) report that groups under the ascendant leaders perform better than the groups under non-ascendant leaders, we do not make a definitive statement of this kind. It is worthwhile to consider another view of power motivation. McClelland (1970) identifies two aspects of n Pow in leaders: personal and institutionalized or socialized powers. Leaders with personalized power dominate for the sake of dominating and personal victory, for them personal achievements are of prime importance. They make their subordinates work for their own selves not for the organizations. They are the likes of feudal lords and exploitative authoritarian leaders. This, obviously, is the dark (negative) side of power and is detrimental both to the growth of the organization and its members. Leaders with institutionalized power, on the other hand, work for the attainment of organizational goals and are concerned with the problems of the organization. These are the people who have a sense of fairness, who take personal responsibility on tasks, and who are mature and open to communication. They provide the structure, drive and support to facilitate goal-oriented group behavior (Steers & Porter, 1987). McClelland (1970) has also reported that leaders with institutionalized power are more effective with respect to subordinate satisfaction and productivity. Also they are more successful than those with personalized face of power.

Need for autonomy has not been so well-studied in the context of leadership. Vroom (1960) notes that n Aut is not found in effective or successful managers. Managers usually work with subordinates and, hence, the need for autonomy has little scope for its manifestation. Bass (1981) notes that n Aut is one of the least well-satisfied needs of the managers.

Need for affiliation too has not been studied much. All the same, McClelland (1970) notes that the subordinates of the managers high on this need feel that they don't have personal responsibility and clarity on organizational procedures and processes; they may also show little pride in their group.

Besides studying the individual needs in isolation, there have been attempts to see the joint effects of two or more needs. Andrews (1967) has compared the need profiles of managers in highly effective or modern (growing and characterized by high morale) and ineffective or traditional (stagnant with no growth) organizations. He reports that upper-level managers in the effective organization are higher on n Ach as compared to their counterparts in the ineffective organizations. Whereas Presidents of both the companies are high on n Pow, the President of the effective organization has moderately high n Ach but the President of the ineffective organization is reported to be low on n Ach. Wainer and Rubin (1969) have found that high n Ach and moderate n Pow of the entrepreneurs are associated with the success of their company. In essence, a combination of n Ach and n Pow of the upper-level managers may predict organizational effectiveness.

Thus, universalists aim at identifying the need dimensions of managers in predicting the effectiveness of leadership. In the contingency framework, Fiedler (1967) begins with the needs of the leader (low and high LPC). Later he (Fiedler, 1978, p. 61) explains LPC as follows: 'If I cannot work with you, if you frustrated my *need* to get the job done, you can't be any good in other respects... The *relationship motivated* individual (who) sees his or her LPC in more positive terms (emphases added).'

The effectiveness of each need is determined by a set of situational variables. Both the universalists and the contingency theorists have the average bias. For them, needs of the leader only are of interest.

Some Conjectures

In the LMX/VDL framework, the focus is on the leader–member dyad and as such any evaluation of the needs or personal orientations has to be done for both of them. It may not be correct to say that only the needs of the leader get manifested and, hence, affect the working of a group.

In the initial stage of role taking, the leader evaluates the relevant motivations of the members with the backdrop of his or her personal needs. We are interested in the *interaction* of personal orientations of the two. Hence we conceive of a typical situation wherein the work orientation (need) of one member in the dyad serves as a situation (or relevant press in Murray's terminology) for the other member. In the exchange framework, some needs of the other member are valuable because they provide for the expression of the leader's needs. Thus, we state the following general hypotheses for empirical verification:

H4.1: Leaders' quality of interaction is a function of the *interaction* of the leaders' and members' personal orientations.

H4.2: Members' quality of interaction and exchange are a function of the *interaction* of the leaders' and members' personal orientations.

Specifically, achievement and independence orientations should follow the similarity rule—that is, if both the leader and the member are high on these dimensions, it should result in a higher or better quality of interaction. Power orientations of both the leader and the member are also of interest. For the leader high on n Pow, a low n Pow member should be the ideal choice for collaboration and vice versa. Besides the combination of the same orientations, other interactions are also expected to affect the quality of interaction. For example, n Ach is expected to be more important in determining perceived contribution than affect, as achievement by definition is more relevant to actual work situations. High n Pow of the leader in combination with the member's orientations can influence both the leader's perceived contribution and affect. For a member there are few chances of the satisfaction of n Pow because of their low power status. Thus, a member high on n Pow is likely to show more affect for a leader low on n Pow, as it gives the members a conducive situation to satisfy their power needs.

Leadership Orientations

The Background

In Chapter 1, it was concluded that the penchant of a leader for a particular style is not refuted. Some leaders are probably more participative than others and some more authoritative. It was also mentioned that the need is to evaluate how the average *and* dyadic leaderships combine. Thus, we attempt a combination of the two.

We begin with the understanding that leaders do indulge in particular ways of leading. These leader behaviors or styles are relatively fixed (at least across subordinates as average theorists presume) and form a part of leaders' orientations towards leading. How these orientations combine with that of subordinates will be taken up later. First, the appropriate orientations of the leader are to be sorted out. For this, we take the Indian theory of and researches on leadership.

In the Indian setting, too, as elsewhere, the phenomenon of leadership has been studied quite extensively. The earlier studies were predominantly concerned with replicating the western studies in the Indian setting. Researchers were interested in ascertaining whether the styles considered effective in the west were effective in India or not (D. Sinha, 1972). The focus of western leadership, after the human relations movement, was on the normative aspect of participative leadership style. The results were mixed and inconclusive. While there are some researchers (e.g., Daftuar & Krishna, 1971; Kakar, 1971; Pandey, 1976; Pestonjee, 1973; A.P. Singh & Pestonjee, 1974) who advocated the effectiveness of participative style, others (e.g., Saiyadain, 1974) advocate the importance of other styles (e.g., autocratic) to be more effective. In the midst of this debate, J.B.P. Sinha (1974) reported that the participative style might fall flat on its face if the cultural settings are not conducive to it. As a consequence, an alternative theory of nurturant-task leadership (NT) was developed. It is worthwhile to note here that Indian studies, in general, and NT formulation in particular, go a step further and identify the values and beliefs of the subordinates. Indian subordinates have been shown to have excessive dependence on their leader (Chattopadhyay, 1975; J.B.P. Sinha, 1980), a readiness to accept their leaders' authority (Kakar, 1971), and a tendency to maintain personalized relationships with their leaders at work (De, 1974; J.B.P. Sinha & M. Sinha, 1974). Thus, an NT leader is effective for those subordinates who want to maintain dependency, a personalized relationship, and a status differential (Ansari, 1990).

Although the need system of the subordinates is identified and the effectiveness of a style is shown to be contingent on it, the evaluation is at a macro level and the subordinates are treated as a collectivity. Though J.B.P. Sinha (1980) identifies the aspect of subordinate maturity as a basis for shift in leadership style (for mature subordinates a shift from NT to participative style of leadership), it is only at the group level. This theory also, like all other average theories, overlooks the leadership process as it occurs within a work-group.

Some Conjectures

In the LMX/VDL framework, the focus is on leader–member dyads. As already mentioned, our interest is in the examination of how leadership orientations of the leaders themselves and the members combine in determining the quality of interaction. It needs to be mentioned here that the objective is not to work out the ideal or effective style but to diagnose how leadership actually occurs in a group.

Thus, we begin with the assumption that whereas leaders have a particular style of leadership, members too have particular and specific attitudes towards these leadership styles. These leadership styles (for the leaders) and the members' preference for these styles are not too different from their general attitudes towards work (like achievement, independence, or power orientations). Whereas n Ach, n Pow, and n Aut (or independence) are broad attitudes towards work, leadership attitudes are specifically relevant to leadership situations. From the member perspective, what we are evaluating is their preference for a style as subordinates. Thus, what we essentially see is a match between the leaders' own styles and members' preference for them. That is, we are looking for a similarity rule in this interaction. This essentially means that if there is a match between leaders' style and members' preference for the style, it is a conducive situation for the two to work amicably. Hence, it should influence perceived contribution positively. Besides creating an efficient working relation, this match (interactions) may produce affective outcomes too. In a reward–cost framework an individual needs to validate his/her opinions, thus the other person's agreement with and support for his/her values becomes rewarding. And hence, it is likely that two individuals with similar values will find it rewarding to work in each other's company (Thibaut & Kelley, 1959).

For this purpose, three leadership styles—authoritarian, nurturant-task and participative—were taken. The leaders described their own styles and the members rated their preference for these styles. In line with the above arguments, the following general hypotheses for the match of leadership orientations (leaders' self-rated style and members' preference for them) are framed.

Since these hypotheses were tested in Study 2, only the members' perception of the quality of interaction were taken. Yet, equivalent hypotheses can also be tested for the leaders' perception of the quality of interaction (which is not done in this report).

H4.3: Members' perceived contribution will be higher when there is a match between leaders' styles and members' preferences.

H4.4: Members affect will be higher when there is a match between leaders' styles and members' preferences.

H4.5: Other measures of quality of exchange (LMX, attention, and latitude) will be higher when there is a match between leaders' style and members' preferences.

Specifically, the interaction of nurturant-task leadership should be more operative for perceived contribution and the interaction of participative leadership should be more pronounced for the members' affect. So far as the authoritarian style is concerned, members might show affect for the leader but the genuinity of the affect is doubtful.

Climate Perceptions

The Background

Before we proceed with our understanding of climate perceptions and its role in determining the quality of exchange, let us briefly take the concept of person–environment interaction. Individuals make a conscious choice of being in an environment or a situation that fits well with their styles and preferences. Thus, interactionist position best describes the world of work (Schneider, 1983). Therefore, the decision of the members whether to collaborate with their leader or not will follow the process of self-selection.

The environment in organizations is conceptualized as climate. The personal orientations were discussed in the first part of this chapter. Now, we present our understanding of climate, for which we begin with Litwin and Stringer's (1968) for whom climate is a measurable concept measured through the perceptions of the people about their work environment which consequently affects their behavior and motivation.

This rather uncomplicated definition does not reveal the controversies involved in the understanding of the concept. Lewin (1951) identified climate as a connecting link between the person (P) and the environment (E). Hence, it can be thought of as a psychological representation of the objective environment. This puts the concept in a precarious position and raises a controversy—whether climate is the objective environment (E) or the individual's perception making it closer to the person (P) (Hellreigel & Slocum, 1974; James & Jones, 1974).

Jones and James (1979) resolve the controversy by further developing the earlier conceptualization made by Litwin and Stringer (1968). Climate, according to them, represents the organizational features and processes which are based on the perceptual descriptions of the organizational members.

For the present study, we are interested in psychological attributes of the climate (*n* Ach, *n* Pow, and *n* Aff) as perceived by organizational members. Hence, we focus on the individual level climate which James and Jones (1974) refer to as 'psychological climate.' According to Jones and James (1979), psychological climate has three essential components. First, it is the individual's perception of the situation, second, these perceptions get interpreted by the individual's frameworks, and finally, they are related to the person's immediate experiences at work.

Having thus defined psychological climate, the next step is to identify different dimensions or aspects of climate. As mentioned above, climate perceptions are more related to the proximal situational factors. Thus, empirically, an investigation of these variables should be useful in the conceptualization of climate. Earlier researches (such as, Hellreigel & Slocum, 1974; Indik, 1968; James & Jones, 1974; Payne & Pugh, 1976; Schneider, 1975; Sells, 1963, 1968) have identified several dimensions like job characteristics (variety, challenge, etc.), social environment (friendliness of the work group), and leader behavior.

Although some of the earlier theorists (e.g., Blake & Mouton, 1964; Lewin, 1951; Likert, 1967; Litwin & Stringer, 1968; McGregor, 1960) recognized the importance of leadership in determining the climate of the organization, in recent times, 'leadership has been all but ignored in this research' (Kozlowski & Doherty, 1989, p. 547). Lewin, Lippitt and White (1939) were indeed the pioneers in this field. They manipulated leadership styles in simulated work-groups and observed the corresponding changes in the climate of the group. In fact, leadership style in their experiment was almost synonymous with the group climate. Litwin and Stringer (1968) created three simulated organizations with three leadership styles—formality, cooperation, and production. Over a period of time, these climates became differentiated depending upon the leader's style. As mentioned earlier, the most immediate phenomena influence the climate perceptions. Consequently, leadership too should be a strong influencing factor. Thus, behaviors of the immediate supervisor may be seen as a representation of a larger organizational climate, also the processes occurring at higher levels get mediated by the immediate supervisor. Thus, the immediate supervisor works as a filter for the individual's work-related experiences (Kozlowski & Doherty, 1989). Litwin and Stringer (1968) also asserted that a particular need orientation of the organization too was a function of the leadership style. They (ibid., p. 101) add:... the climates and the leadership styles designed to create them can be characterized as power-related (Organization A), affiliative (Organization B), and achieving (Organization C).

In essence, we can say that particular need orientations of the organization for the members are related to their leaders' behavior. Conversely, the need orientations of the organization, in general, can be equated with the immediate leader's style. Thus, the members' perceptions of organizational climate are their (the members') leaders' manifested style of working.

Some Conjectures

In the LMX/VDL framework, we again take the interactionists' perspective. The climate perceptions of the member are the leaders' working style. These climate orientations though are related to the leaders' own styles and orientations, they cannot be equated with them. Climate is the perception of the member and hence probably represents the *actual* working condition for the members. After all, the leader too is a part of the organization and only partly reflects his or her own orientations.

Hence, these climate perceptions, in conjunction with the members' own attributes or orientations towards work should determine the members' perception of the quality of exchange but the same interaction for the leader (personal attributes and climate) is less relevant in determining his or her interaction with the subordinate. This leads us to the following hypotheses.

H4.6: Members' perceived contribution will be higher if there is a match between their personal orientations and climate perceptions.

H4.7: Members' affect will be higher if there is a match between their personal orientations and climate perceptions.

H4.8: Other measures of quality of exchange (LMX, attention, and latitude) from the members' perspective will be higher if there is a match between their personal orientations and climate perceptions.

Thus, essentially, climate is expected to play a significant role in determining the members' quality of exchange (or interaction) without affecting leaders' quality of exchange (or interaction). Further, since 'people select themselves into and out of situations based on the general fit of themselves to the situation' (Schneider, 1983, p. 13), the interaction of personal orientations and climate is expected to be significant. However collaboration on unstructured tasks is voluntary on the members' part and they have the option of not collaborating with the members. Therefore, the person–environment interaction in this case will not follow the usual rule where members are bound to work with and according to the leader (e.g., for contractual work).

Results

Personal Orientations and Quality of Interaction

Three match orientations (power, achievement, and independence) of the leaders and members were taken. The hypotheses are tested through the application of 2 × 2 ANOVA. The personal attributes of the leader and the member are divided into 'low' and 'high' by splitting at the median. Nine interactions are tested for every hypothesis.

Leaders' Perception of the Quality of Interaction

The first hypothesis (H4.1) is tested only in Study 1. So far as the perceived contribution of the leader is concerned, none of the interactions is significant. The significance of F-ratios can be seen in Table 4.1.

Affect of the leader too is not predicted by the interaction of the personal attributes of the two. Only in one case is there a

Table 4.1

Significance of F-ratios—Leaders' Quality of Interaction as a Function
of Interaction of Leaders' and Members' Personal Orientations
(Study 1)

PR/CR	F-ratios Perceived Contribution	Affect
LA× MA	ns	ns
LA × MI	ns	.04
LA × MP	ns	ns
LI × MA	ns	ns
LI × MI	ns	ns
LI × MP	ns	ns
LP ×MA	ns	ns
LP × MI	ns	ns
LP × MP	ns	ns

Note: $df = 1/148$; LA, LI, and LP are, respectively, leaders' Achievement, Independ-
ence, and Power Orientations; MA, MI, and MP are, respectively, members'
Achievement, Independence, and Power Orientations; PR = Predictors; CR =
Criterion; ns = not significant.

significant interaction—that too marginally. Leader's achievement
orientation interacts with the member's independence orientation
in predicting the former's affect, $F(1,148) = 4.29$. To see the direction and exact nature of this relationship, members' independence
and leaders' achievement orientations were divided into low and
high categories (median split). Thus we had leaders' mean Affect
scores for four combinations of leader–member orientations—
(*i*) low achievement of the leader and low independence of the
member ($M = 15.30$, $N = 42$); (*ii*) low achievement of the leader
and high independence of the member ($M = 15.77$, $N = 39$);
(*iii*) high achievement of the leader and low independence of the
member ($M = 9.11$, $N = 28$); and (*iv*) high achievement of the
leader and high independence of the member ($M = 15.21$, $N =
43$). A high achievement oriented leader has the highest affect for a
member low on independence and the lowest affect for a member
high on independence. If at all the personal attributes of the two
are important (which is doubtful), probably a high achievement-
oriented leader likes more dependent (less independent) subordinates, as the subordinates' dependence may be a sense of achievement

for the leader who does not like a highly independent subordinate. Also, since a leader has to work with a group, an achievement-oriented leader would have a liking for such subordinates who depend on him or her for all the decisions. These subordinates also give the leader the satisfaction of taking the credit for the work done (which probably the leader only does because of high *n* Ach).

Thus, with the exception of one interaction (of the possible 18), hypothesis (H4.1) stands unsubstantiated.

Members' Perception of the Quality of Interaction and Exchange

The next hypothesis (H4.2) is concerned with the members' quality of interaction and its determinants. Determinants of perceived contribution and affect of the members are studied in both the studies (Study 1 and 2). The results of these studies are contained in Tables 4.2 and 4.3 respectively. These results are discussed side by side.

Only one interaction significantly determines the members' perceived contribution in Study 1 (see Table 4.2). The achievement orientation of both the leader and the member jointly influences

Table 4.2

Significance of F-ratios—Members' Quality of Exchange as a Function of Interaction of Leaders' and Members' Personal Orientations (Study 1)

PR/CR	Perceived Contribution	Affect	LMX
MA x LA	.03	ns	ns
MA x LI	ns	ns	ns
MA x LP	ns	ns	ns
MI x LA	ns	ns	ns
MI x LI	ns	ns	ns
MI x LP	ns	ns	ns
MI x LA	ns	ns	ns
MP x LI	ns	ns	ns
MP x LP	ns	ns	ns

Note: df = 1/148; LA, LI, and LP are, respectively, leaders' Achievement, Independence, and Power Orientations; MA, MI, and MP are, respectively, members' Achievement, Independence, and Power Orientations; PR = Predictors; CR = Criterion; ns = not significant.

the member's perceived contribution in this study, F (1,148) = 4.94. Again, to see the direction and exact nature of this relationship, the leader's and member's achievement orientation were divided into low and high categories. Thus, we have members' mean scores on perceived contribution for each one of these combinations. (High achievement of both, $M = 26.56$, $N = 39$; high achievement of leader and low of member, $M = 26.34$, $N = 32$; low achievement of the leader and high achievement of the member, $M = 22.88$, $N = 41$; low achievement of both $M = 25.51$, $N = 40$). It can be seen that a high achievement-oriented member's perceived contribution is maximum for a high achievement-oriented leader, whereas for a low n Ach leader the perceived contribution of the same member (high n Ach) is minimum. This clearly seems to be following the similarity rule. If both of them are high on achievement motivation, both of them set targets of moderate risk, both believe in the completion of the task, and, in essence, each provides the required atmosphere for the other to work. This situation becomes more conducive for the member because the leader can impose his or her way of working on the members but members cannot do the same for the leader. In Study 2 also, only one of the interactions is significant. Leader's power orientation interacts with members' independence to determine the member's perceived contribution. A low independence-oriented member shows maximum perceived contribution ($M = 23.96$, $N = 27$) for a leader high on power orientation, whereas high independence-oriented member perceives the contribution of a high power-oriented leader to be the least ($M = 20.50$, $N = 24$). This follows a complementarity rule. A less independent (more dependent) member gives in to the leaders' power orientation and the two get along well together. On the other hand, a member high on independence orientation does not give in to the power-motivated leader.

As regards the affect of the member, none of the interactions either in Study 1 (see Table 4.4 and Table 4.6 for the significance of F-ratios and means, respectively) or in Study 2 (see Table 4.3 for significance of F-ratios) is significant. Thus, only two interactions (of the possible 36) significantly predict the quality of interaction from the members' perspective.

Finally, other measures of quality of exchange are considered. LMX is taken up in Study 1 and Attention and Latitude are examined in Study 2. LMX is not predicted by any interaction (see Table 4.2 for significance of F-ratios). The significance of interaction results (F-ratios) for attention and latitude (both in Study 2) are given in Table 4.3. It is evident that none of the interactions for attention reaches its significance level. However, for latitude (Study 2), one interaction—power orientation of the leader and independence orientation of the member—is significant (see Table 4.3 for significance of F-ratios). It is clear that a low independence-oriented member gets (or perceives) maximum latitude from a leader high on power, whereas a high independence-oriented member gets minimum latitude from the power-oriented leader. The finding is identical with that of perceived contribution and the explanation, too, may be the same. Thus, in general, hypothesis H4.2 also stands rejected in our present investigations.

Table 4.3

Significance of F-ratios—Members' Quality of Exchange as a Function of Interaction of Leaders' and Members' Personal Orientations (Study 2)

PR/CR	Perceived Contribution	Affect	Attention	Latitude
MA × LA	ns	ns	ns	ns
MA × LI	ns	ns	ns	ns
MA × LP	ns	ns	ns	ns
MI × LA	ns	ns	ns	ns
MI × LI	ns	ns	ns	ns
MI × LP	.05	ns	ns	.05
MP × LA	ns	ns	ns	ns
MP × LI	ns	ns	ns	ns
MP × LP	ns	ns	ns	ns

Note: $df = 1/92$; LA, LI, and LP are, respectively, leaders' Achievement, Independence, and Power Orientations; MA, MI, and MP are, respectively, members' Achievement, Independence, and Power Orientations, PR = Predictors; CR = Criterion; ns = not significant.

Comments

Barring a very few (almost negligible) interactions, the personal attributes of the leader and the member do not statistically interact to determine the quality of interaction (also quality of exchange), neither for the member perspective nor for the leader perspective.

Whereas the leaders' perspective is evaluated only in Study 1, members' perspective is evaluated in both the studies. Almost identical results from both the perspectives provide validity and support to the present findings. Also, it is not only the quality of interaction measures that are specifically developed in this study that are not determined by this interaction but the other measures (LMX, attention, and latitude) also are not. Finally, the fact that results of both the studies yielded the same results confirms the validity of the findings. This shows that, no matter what measures of exchange we take, they seem to be rather independent of the interaction of the personal attributes of the two. In view of the fact that interaction hypotheses do not receive support from the present two sets of data, some additional comments are in order.

To begin with, leaders and members evaluate their own attitudes towards work. It is not necessary that the perception of one's own personal orientations match with the other's perception of the self. We presumed that the evaluation of one's own attributes is an objective evaluation and others also perceive them to be the same. Thus, a more viable and practical hypothesis will be the evaluation of one's own personal attributes and perception of the same attributes in the relevant other.

Second, probably the personal attributes of the two are not so important in determining the interaction between a leader and a member. What we are measuring are very personal attitudes (though towards work) and they may not play such an important role in leader–member interactions. These attitudes probably may be operative in very close and intimate relationships, like spouse selection (Peterson, 1977, 1979), where one partner actually constitutes total climate or environment for the other. The leader–member interactions are primarily work relations which operate in the backdrop of organizational settings. Hence, the broader organizational variables, which are relevant to the leadership situation, probably are more important. This does not mean that the motives and attitudes of the two are not important. They are important but only in interaction with other more direct variables such as climate. Thus, in the initial stage of role taking, the leader does evaluate the members' relevant motives and orientations, but the relevance of these is determined by other factors (e.g., the nature of the job). The members' choice of the leader, too, may be guided by other practical considerations.

Finally, our conception of interaction is based on statistical interaction. As Schneider (1983, p. 8) notes, 'in field settings ... extremes of person variables are not typically observed,' this effect gets compounded when the sample size is relatively small. In both the studies, the number of leaders is much less (67 in Study 1 and 26 in Study 2). This could also be a probable reason for the lack of interaction. Lack of statistical interaction, however, (measured through ANOVA or multiple regression) does not necessarily mean lack of interaction of variables in real-life situations (Schneider, 1983).

Next, we look at the results of leadership orientations—leaders' styles and members' preferences for these styles.

Leadership Styles and Quality of Interaction

The results of hypothesis H4.3 are reported in Tables 4.4 and 4.5. Of the three match interactions, two significantly predict members' perceived contribution. The authoritarian and participative leadership orientations show significant interactions. The analysis indicates (see Table 4.5) that those members who have a high preference for authoritarian style of leadership perceive a high authoritarian leaders' contribution (PC) to be maximum on the job. On the other hand, the same contribution is minimum when the leader is authoritarian but the member has low preference for authoritarian leadership. As was mentioned earlier, in high quality dyads, the interdependence between the leader and the member was very high. For the member this dependence is crucial; on the one hand, when it can help the member in career progress, on the other hand, because of incompatibility, it might stagnate all growth at the same time. Thus, it is unlikely that a member with little preference for authoritarian leadership will collaborate with the leader on unstructured tasks. Such members may maintain a contractual relationship with the leader. Consequently, they perceive leaders' contribution to be less on the job. Only those members who have a preference for authoritarian leadership will collaborate with authoritarian leaders on the job.

A similar interaction for participative orientations too was significant. It can be seen from Table 4.5 that members who have a low preference for the participative style perceive a low participative

Table 4.4
F-ratios and Their Significance—Members' Quality of Exchange as a Function of Interaction of Leadership Orientations (Study 2)

CR/PR	LS(F) X SP(F)	LS(N) X SP(N)	LS(P) X SP(P)
Perceived Contribution	7.99[a]	3.36	5.05[b]
Affect	4.68[b]	2.80	3.67[b]
Attention	18.82[a]	7.31[a]	8.67[a]
Latitude	15.07[a]	7.76[a]	5.47[a]

Note: Df = 1/92. LS = Leadership style of the leaders; SP = Style preference of the members; F = Authoritarian style; N = Nurturant-task style; P = Participative style; CR = Criterion; PR = Predictor; [a] = $p < .01$; [b] = $p < .05$.

leaders' contribution to be the most. The same contribution is minimum when the leader is low on participation but the member has a high preference for participative style. A low–low match in this case is understandable, since the participative leader is more

Table 4.5
Mean Scores—Members' Perceived Contribution as a Function of Leaders' and Members' Leadership Orientations (Study 2)

SP		SP(F)		SP(N)		SP(P)	
	LS	LOW	HIGH	LOW	HIGH	LOW	HIGH
LS(N)	LOW			23.83 (23)	21.20 (15)		
	HIGH			20.35 (34)	23.42 (24)		
LS(P)	LOW					24.50 (28)	18.23 (22)
	HIGH					22.33 (24)	22.59 (22)
LS(F)	LOW	23.74 (23)	21.00 (31)				
	HIGH	18.59 (17)	24.28 (25)				

Note: LS = Leadership Style; SP = Style Preference; N = Nurturant-task; P = Participative; F = Authoritarian. Numbers in parantheses indicate the number of cases.

concerned with the feelings of the subordinates and less concerned with the job. It is likely that actual contribution to work is not so much predicted by a high–high match. For the lowest contribution, it is a case of mismatch because low in participation does not necessarily mean (at all times) high on job or task. A failure for the nurturant-task interaction to yield significant results is difficult to explain.

The results for hypothesis H4.4 are reported in Tables 4.4 and 4.6. Here also the same two interactions—authoritarian and participative—are significant (Table 4.4). An examination of Table 4.6 reveals that members who have a low preference for the authoritarian style have maximum affect for leaders low on authoritarian style. Also members who have a low preference for the authoritarian style have minimum affect for leaders high on authoritarian style. Although this finding also follows the similarity hypothesis, it is interesting to compare this result with that of perceived

Table 4.6

Mean Scores—Members' Affect as a Function of Leaders' and Members' Leadership Orientations (Study 2)

SP		SP(F)		SP(N)		SP(P)	
	LS	LOW	HIGH	LOW	HIGH	LOW	HIGH
LS(N)	LOW			18.33 (23)	14.21 (15)		
	HIGH			18.33 (34)	19.48 (24)		
LS(P)	LOW					18.43 (28)	11.09 (22)
	HIGH					18.27 (22)	20.17
LS(F)	LOW	19.35 (23)	16.55 (31)				
	HIGH	14.00 (17)	18.00 (25)				

Note: Same as Table 4.4.

Table 4.7

Mean Scores—Members' Attention as a Function of Leaders' and Members' Leadership Orientations (Study 2)

SP		SP(F)		SP(N)		SP(P)	
LS		LOW	HIGH	LOW	HIGH	LOW	HIGH
LS(N)	LOW			16.71 (23)	13.00 (15)		
	HIGH			14.20 (34)	16.78 (24)		
LS(P)	LOW					17.29 (28)	10.55 (22)
	HIGH					16.04 (24)	15.50 (22)
LS(F)	LOW	16.96 (23)	14.32 (31)				
	HIGH	10.47 (17)	17.22 (25)				

Note: Same as Table 4.4.

contribution (PC). For PC, a high–high match is more important. This shows that a high preference for authoritarian style is limited to working relationships. That is, affect or liking is not predicted so much by high preference for authoritarian style. Affect is predictably low for a high authoritarian leader especially of members who have a low preference for the authoritarian style.

Participative interaction, too, was significant (Table 4.4). Members who have a high preference for participative style have the highest affect for leaders high on the participative style. In addition, the same members have least affect for a leader low on participation (Table 4.6). The results follow the similarity rule but again it is interesting to compare these findings with those of perceived contribution. Leaders' participation (high or low) significantly influences members' quality of interaction but affect is predicted better by a high–high match and a low–low match better explains perceived contribution. Thus high participative style of the leader is more operative for the affect dimension.

Members' Attention

The *F*-ratios and their significance level for the attention dimension are given in Table 4.4. The means for the same are given in Table 4.7. An overall observation of the statistical interactions shows that the interaction for authoritarian and participative styles is almost identical to perceived contribution.

So far as the authoritarian style interaction is concerned, attention is maximum when both the leadership style and style preference (by the members) are high. Attention is lowest when the leader is high on authoritarian style but the member has a low preference for the same style.

For the participative style interaction, attention is maximum when both these orientations are high but attention is minimum when the member has a high preference for participative style but the leader is low on this style.

Additionally, the interaction of nurturant-task interaction also shows significant results. Attention is the highest when both these orientations are high and it (attention) is minimum when the members have a high preference for nurturant-task style and the leader is low on it.

Clearly, a match of leadership orientations leads to more attention and a mismatch leads to less attention. This effect gets more pronounced for participative and nurturant-task orientations, as these orientations are more directly related to the exchange dimension of attention.

Members' Latitude

The *F*-ratios and their significance for latitide are given in Table 4.4 and the means are reported in Table 4.8. All the three interactions are significant.

For the authoritarian interaction, latitude is maximum when both these orientations are high but it (latitude) is minimum when the leader is high on authoritarian style but the members have a low preference for this style.

Leadership orientations towards participative style also show a significant interaction. Strangely enough, latitude is maximum when both these orientations are low and it (latitude) is the least

Table 4.8
Mean Scores—Members' Latitude as a Function of Leaders' and Members' Leadership Orientations (Study 2)

SP		SP(F)		SP(N)		SP(P)	
	LS	LOW	HIGH	LOW	HIGH	LOW	HIGH
LS(N)	LOW			13.91 (23)	11.07 (15)		
	HIGH			11.85 (34)	13.54 (24)		
LS(P)	LOW					13.82 (28)	10.68 (22)
	HIGH					12.62 (24)	13.14 (22)
LS(F)	LOW	13.36 (23)	11.74 (31)				
	HIGH	10.41 (17)	14.74 (25)				

Note: Same as Table 4.4.

when the leader is low on this style but the member has a high preference for this style.

Finally, the interaction of nurturant-task orientations, too, is significant. Latitude is maximum when both the orientations are low and it is minimum when members have a high preference for this style but the leader's preference is low.

Again, a match of leadership orientations leads to more latitude and a mismatch leads to less latitude. However, a match of low–low participative style predicting maximum latitude is unexpected because latitude given by the leader should be a direct function of the participative style of the leader.

Comments

A general support for the hypotheses relating to leadership orientations shows that the behaviors or attitudes directly related to the leadership situation are instrumental in determining the quality of exchange in dyads.

We begin with the average leadership styles of the leader which are relatively stable orientations and which hold true across all subordinates. But the actual leader–member interactions in a work-group are affected as much by the members' orientations (preferences) towards these leadership styles as by the leaders' own style. Thus, a study of the interaction of the two leads to a better understanding of the process.

The failure of authoritarian leaders in the average framework can be attributed to some other variables. First of all, not many subordinates are likely to prefer the authoritarian style of leadership. It can be seen in Chapter 2 that the mean for authoritarian preference is lowest (2.32) as compared to nurturant-task (3.33) and participative (3.35). Thus, the general average assumptions are not refuted totally but an interactive (leaders' styles and members' preference) hypothesis is a better predictor of the work-unit functioning.

Next, we focus on traditional person–environment interaction in predicting quality of exchange.

Climate and Personal Orientations Determining Quality of Interaction

This set of hypotheses (H4.6, H4.7 and H4.8) were statistically tested through hierarchical multiple regression analysis wherein perceived contribution, affect and other measures of LMX are taken as dependent variables and for each one of them the interaction between climate perception and personal orientation is taken as an independent variable. We present the results in sequence.

Study 1 Results

Members' Perceived Contribution

The beta coefficients and R^2 change are presented in Table 4.9. As is evident, five interactions significantly determine perceived contribution; of which four are highly significant ($p < .01$). The mean scores of perceived contribution as a function of this interaction are shown in Table 4.10.

Table 4.9
Hierarchical Regression Results—Members' Quality of Exchange as a Function of the Interaction of Their Personal Orientations and Climate Perceptions (Study 1)

PR CR	Perceived Contribution	Affect	LMX
MA x CA	(.22[a], .05)	(.21[a], .04)	(.22, .05)
MA x CI	(.01, .00)	(.08, .01)	(−.02, .00)
MA x CP	(.17[a], .03)	(.16[b], .03)	(.16[b], .03)
MI x CA	(.22[a], .04)	(.11, .01)	(.20[b], .04)
MI x CI	(−.10, .01)	(.16[b], .02)	(−.06, .00)
MI x CP	(.17[b], .03)	(.07, .00)	(.17[b], .03)
MP x CA	(.25[a], .06)	(.22[a], .05)	(.21, .04)
MP x CI	(−.04, .00)	(−.11, .01)	(−.06, .00)
MP x CP	(.11, .01)	(.12, .01)	(.19[b], .03)

Note: $N = 152$; a $p < .01$; b $p < .05$; MA, MI, and MP are, respectively, members' Achievement, Independence, and Power Orientations; CA, CI, and CP are, respectively, members' climate perception for Achievement, Independence, and Power Orientations; PR = Predictor; CR = Criterion; Figures in parantheses are beta coefficients and R^2 change, respectively.

Table 4.10
Mean Scores—Members' Perceived Contribution as a Function of Members' Personal Orientations and Climate Perceptions (Study 1)

MC	M	MC(P) LOW	MC(P) HIGH	MC(A) LOW	MC(A) HIGH	MC(I) LOW	MC(I) HIGH
M(P)	LOW	6.30	4.74	3.89*	4.91	4.55	6.10
	HIGH	6.07	5.55	4.23	6.63	4.40	4.88
M(A)	LOW	5.76	5.37	5.49	4.50	5.04	6.20
	HIGH	5.80	3.40	4.20	5.86	4.67	5.47
M(I)	LOW	5.22	5.73	4.87	5.20	3.90	6.00
	HIGH	5.26	4.12	3.72	6.35	4.69	5.34

Note: $N = 152$; M = Members' Personal Orientations; MC = Members' Climate Perceptions; A = Achievement; I = Independence; P = Power; *Predicted mean scores (Winer, 1971).

First of all, the achievements of both the members and the climate interact significantly. Perceived contribution is maximum for members who are high on n Ach and are working in a high achievement-oriented climate; it (perceived contribution) is minimum when the member is high on achievement orientation but the climate is low on the same need. Clearly, a match between the predictors predicts high perceived contribution and a mismatch predicts low perceived contribution. Obviously, a high achievement-oriented climate facilitates the n Ach of the members and a high n Ach member finds the climate conducive for work and, hence, assigns a high rating to perceived contribution. On the other hand, a high n Ach member will naturally perceive a low n Ach climate to be less efficient. Besides, a low n Ach climate does not provide enough environmental presses for the members' needs to be satisfied and the members refrain from collaborating on unstructured tasks.

Next, the achievement orientation of the member and power orientation of the climate also show a significant interaction effect. Perceived contribution is maximum when the member is high on achievement orientation and the climate is low on power. The same contribution is minimum when the member is high on achievement and the climate is high on power. A high power-oriented climate excessively controls and guides the members' activities leaving little scope for the members to satisfy their achievement orientation. On the other hand, a low power-oriented climate, by not doing so, leaves enough scope for the member to satisfy his or her achievement needs. Thus, in the former situation, the member does not collaborate whereas in the latter situation he or she does.

Members' power orientation and achievement orientation of the climate also yield significant interaction results. A member high on power orientation shows maximum perceived contribution in a high achievement-oriented climate, but the contribution (perceived) is minimum when a low power-oriented member works in a low achievement-oriented climate. This finding is rather difficult to explain. It is really hard to explain how achievement orientation of the climate facilitates the power orientation of the members.

Next, independence orientation of the members and power orientation of the climate interact significantly to predict members' perceived contribution. It can be seen that the perceived contribution is maximum for a low independence-oriented member who is working in a high power-oriented climate, and it (perceived contribution) is minimum when the member is high on independence and climate too is high on power. Collaboration in this case seems to be following a complementarity rule. Very clearly, a high power-oriented climate guides and controls the activities of the members, so that the members do not have to do anything independently. Thus, such a climate is a boon for all those members who avoid independence (low on independence) and they work best (and hence collaborate) in such a climate. The same climate (i.e., low independence oriented) will clash with the members' needs if they (the members) are high on independence. In such a situation members will limit their contribution to contractual tasks only.

Finally, independence orientation of the members and achievement orientation of the climate also provide significant interaction results. Perceived contribution is maximum when a high independence-oriented member works in a high achievement-oriented climate, but it is the lowest when the same (high independence-oriented) member works in a low achievement-oriented climate. Achievement-oriented climate probably demands results and does not hamper the individual's independence much. Hence a high independence-oriented member works well in such a climate, collaborates more with the leader, and has more perceived contribution. At the same time it is hard to explain, how a low achievement-oriented climate restricts members' independence.

Members' Affect

The results for affect revealed four significant interactions. The beta coefficients and R^2 square change of the same are depicted in Table 4.9. The mean scores are given in Table 4.11.

First, the members' and the climates' achievement orientations interact significantly to predict the members' affect. Affect is highest when both these orientations are high and is lowest when the climate is high on achievement orientation and the member himself or herself is low on achievement orientation. It is obvious that the member will have a liking for a climate that facilitates his or her personal dispositions. Thus, an achievement-oriented member shows a high liking (affect) when the climate too is high on achievement orientation. In the same vein, a member low on achievement

Table 4.11

Mean Scores—Members' Affect as a Function of Members' Personal Orientations and Climate Perceptions (Study 1)

MC		MC(P)		MC(A)		MC(I)	
	M	LOW	HIGH	LOW	HIGH	LOW	HIGH
M(P)	LOW	4.00	1.94	1.48*	2.34	2.05	3.75
	HIGH	3.67	3.67	2.30	4.83	1.70	3.42
M(A)	LOW	3.52	1.28	4.17	1.40	3.24	2.70
	HIGH	4.33	4.23	2.70	4.43	3.07	4.09
M(I)	LOW	3.60	2.52	2.67	3.05	3.03	3.31
	HIGH	3.77	3.05	2.75	4.20	2.65	3.72

Note: Same as Table 4.10.

orientation is very likely to find a high achievement-oriented climate pushy. Consequently, the member shows low affect.

Second, the achievement orientation of the member and power orientation of the climate show significant interaction results. It can be seen that affect is maximum when the member is high on achievement orientation and the climate is low on power. In contrast, affect is minimum when the member is low on achievement orientation but the climate is high on power. This shows that affect is a direct function of the member's own achievement orientation and it is an inverse function of the power orientation of the climate, when the two orientations are taken together. A climate, low on power orientation, gives the members the power (freedom) to satisfy his or her achievement needs. Hence, the member shows a high affect. But when the member is low on achievement orientation but the climate controls the activities of the members, members find the climate pushy and domineering, and show a low affect.

Third, the achievement orientation of the climate and power orientation of the self (members) interact significantly to determine affect. Affect is highest when both these orientations are high and is lowest when both these orientations are low—a finding once again difficult to explain.

Finally, the independence orientations of both the members and the climate interact significantly. Affect is highest when both these orientations are high and is lowest when the member is high and the climate is low on independence. Clearly, affect follows the similarity rule. A climate high on independence provides the necessary press for a member to satisfy his or her independence needs. The affect obviously is low when a member high on independence orientation works in a climate that gives less autonomy.

Study 2 Results

Members' Perceived Contribution

Three interaction effects significantly predicted members' perceived contribution in this study. The beta coefficients and R^2 change can be looked up in Table 4.12 and the mean scores of perceived contribution for the interaction terms are provided in Table 4.13. Of the three interactions, two were the same as in Study 1.

Table 4.12

Hierarchical Regression Results—Members' Quality of Exchange as a Function of the Interaction of Their Personal Orientations and Climate Perceptions (Study 2)

PR CR	Perceived Contribution	Affect	Attention	Latitude
MA x CA	$(-.23^b, .05)$	$(-.21^b, .04)$	$(-.26^a, .06)$	$(-.23^b, .04)$
MA x CI	$(-.23^b, .05)$	$(-.25^a, .06)$	$(.31^a, .09)$	$(-.26^a, .06)$
MA x CP	$(.10, .01)$	$(.06, .00)$	$(.11, .01)$	$(.09, .00)$
MP x CA	$(-.16, .02)$	$(-.14, .02)$	$(-.19^b, .03)$	$(-.24^b, .05)$
MP x CI	$(.00, .00)$	$(-.05, .00)$	$(-.11, .01)$	$(-.21^b, .04)$
MP x CP	$(-.05, .001)$	$(-.19^b, .03)$	$(-.12, .01)$	$(-.19, .03)$
MI x CA	$(.03, .00)$	$(-.06, .00)$	$(-.06, .00)$	$(.00, .00)$
MI x CI	$(.12, .01)$	$(.02, .00)$	$(.07, .00)$	$(.15, .02)$
MI x CP	$(-.21^b, .04)$	$(-.16, .03)$	$(-.17, .03)$	$(-.27^a, .07)$

Note: $N = 96$; a $p < .01$; b $p < .05$; MA, MP, and MI are respectively, members' Achievement, Power and Independence Orientations; CA, CP, and CI are respectively, members' perception of climate for Achievement, Power, and Independence Orientations; PR = Predictor, CR = Criterion; Figures in parantheses are beta coefficients and R^2 change respectively.

Table 4.13

Mean Scores—Members' Perceived Contribution as a Function of Members' Personal Orientations and Climate Perceptions (Study 2)

MC		MC(P)		MC(A)		MC(I)	
	M	LOW	HIGH	LOW	HIGH	LOW	HIGH
M(P)	LOW	5.40	2.60	4.21*	5.71	4.50	5.47
	HIGH	3.40	2.70	2.85	4.50	2.90	3.96
M(A)	LOW	3.50	2.13	4.50	4.87	2.70	2.80
	HIGH	3.40	4.53	2.73	6.40	3.83*	4.45
M(I)	LOW	3.93	4.60	3.47	5.25	3.07	4.55
	HIGH	5.70	2.65	2.80	6.00	2.63	4.92

Note: $N = 96$; for abbreviations, see Table 4.10.

The first interaction that was clearly repeated in this study was the one between the achievement orientations of the members and the climate. It can be seen that a high–high match predicts maximum perceived contribution, whereas for a high n Ach member working in a low achievement-oriented climate (a mismatch), the perceived contribution is minimum. This result replicates that of Study 1 and provides further strength to this particular interaction.

Next, the independence orientation of the members and power orientation of the climate (as in Study 1) yield a significant interaction. That is, maximum perceived contribution is predicted when a member high on independence orientation works in a climate low on power orientation. But perceived contribution is minimum when both are high on their respective orientations. This result too is an exact replication of Study 1, thereby strengthening the importance of this interaction.

Finally, a third interaction which is new to this study is of interest. Perceived contribution is significantly predicted by the interaction of member's achievement orientation and the climate's independence orientation. Maximum perceived contribution is predicted when both these orientations are high, and minimum perceived contribution results when both are low. A climate high on independence orientation gives the members enough freedom to set their goals and choose their work pattern which helps a high n Ach person. Thus, a high–high cell predicting high contribution seems justified.

Members' Affect

Three interactions significantly influenced the affect of the members. Beta coefficients and R^2 change are given in Table 4.12, and the means of interaction terms are given in Table 4.14. Of the three significant interactions, only one was repeated from Study 1.

Table 4.14

Mean Scores—Members' Affect as a Function of Members' Personal Orientations and Climate Perceptions (Study 2)

MC		MC(P)		MC(A)		MC(I)	
	M	LOW	HIGH	LOW	HIGH	LOW	HIGH
M(P)	LOW	2.40	1.85	3.13*	4.44	1.90	4.25
	HIGH	3.40	1.20	1.85	3.20	1.83	2.86
M(A)	LOW	3.10	3.87	3.20	1.33	1.70	1.40
	HIGH	2.40	3.09	3.60	4.00	2.93*	3.40
M(I)	LOW	3.00	3.70	1.87	4.35	1.60	3.85
	HIGH	3.70	2.35	2.35	4.17	2.03	3.52

Note: $N = 96$; for abbreviations, see Table 4.10.

Just as in Study 1, the achievement orientations of the members themselves and the climate show a significant interaction. It can be seen that affect is highest when both these orientations are high but it is lowest when the member is low on achievement but the climate is high on achievement orientation. This result is identical with that of Study 1.

The next significant interaction is between the achievement orientation of the members and the independence orientation of the climate. Affect is highest when both are high and it is lowest when the member is low on achievement orientation but the climate is high on independence. Clearly, a member with high n Ach prefers to have autonomy (independence) on jobs and shows more affect for the leader in such a case. It is hard to explain the results for low affect. Probably, a member who is low on achievement orientation looks for more order and control in the climate. However, if the climate lacks such order and control, affect becomes low.

Finally, the power orientations of the members and the climate show significant interaction results. When the member is high on power and the climate is low on power, the affect is maximum. But the affect is minimum when both are high on power orientation. Clearly, affect follows the complementarity rule. A member who likes to dominate gets enough opportunity to do so when the climate does not control and guide his or her activities. The member in this case shows maximum affect. When the same member works in a high power-oriented climate, the collaboration is minimum and so is affect.

Other Measures of Exchange

As was mentioned in Chapter 3, other measures of leader–member exchange were included in the studies. The interaction of personal orientations and climate as a determinant of these measures, too, was tested. The three additional measures that were included were: LMX (Leader–Member Exchange), Attention, and Latitude—the first was included in Study 1 and the last two were included in Study 2. All three represented the members' perspective only.

Members' LMX

Four interactions significantly predicted LMX. The beta coefficients and R^2 change are given in Table 4.9 and the means are given in Table 4.15.

Members' achievement orientation and power orientation of the climate interact significantly in predicting LMX. The LMX is maximum when members' achievement orientation is high and the climate is low on power orientation, whereas LMX is minimum when both are high. As mentioned before, a climate low on power does not interfere with the activities of the members. For a high n Ach member, such a climate is a boon; hence, it leads to more collaboration and high LMX. But when the climate controls and directs (high n power) the activities of the members, the members do not get

Table 4.15

Mean Scores—Members' LMX as a Function of Members' Personal Orientations and Climate Perceptions (Study 1)

MC		MC(P)		MC(A)		MC(I)	
	M	LOW	HIGH	LOW	HIGH	LOW	HIGH
M(P)	LOW	3.20	2.97	2.29*	2.71	2.15	3.25
	HIGH	3.60	2.43	2.40	3.37	2.50	2.86
M(A)	LOW	3.12	3.07	3.23	2.07	2.64	3.40
	HIGH	3.17	1.88	2.95	3.37	2.93	3.27
M(I)	LOW	2.94	2.92	2.67	2.80	2.35	3.04
	HIGH	3.13	2.28	2.27	3.52	2.57	3.14

Note: Same as Table 4.10.

enough opportunities to satisfy their achievement needs. Consequently, LMX is minimal.

Second, the power orientations of both—the members and the climate—also show a significant interaction. LMX is found to be maximum when a member is high on need for power and works in a climate which is low on need for power. LMX is minimum when the same member (high *n* Pow) works in a climate that too is power oriented. Thus, LMX clearly follows the complementarity rule, as mentioned before.

Climate seems to interact significantly with both independence and achievement orientations of the members in predicting LMX. The LMX is maximum when both are high and it is minimum when the member is high on independence but the climate is low on achievement. The result eludes explanation. The results will be logical if we make an assumption that an achievement-oriented climate gives enough autonomy to the members—a pure conjecture.

Finally, the independence orientation of the members and power orientation of the climate interact significantly to predict LMX. The LMX is maximum when members' independence orientation is high and the climate is low on power, whereas LMX is minimum when both are high. Clearly, collaboration is based on the complementarity rule.

Members' Attention

Three interactions significantly predicted members' attention. Beta coefficients and R^2 change are given in Table 4.12 and mean scores can be seen in Table 4.16.

Table 4.16

Mean Scores—Members' Attention as a Function of Members'
Personal Orientations and Climate Perceptions (Study 2)

MC		MC(P)		MC(A)		MC(I)	
M	LOW	HIGH	LOW	HIGH	LOW	HIGH
M(P) LOW	3.80	1.60	1.95	4.31	2.50	4.20
HIGH	2.60	1.75	2.61	2.70	2.10	2.88
M(A) LOW	2.90	1.73	2.73	2.70	2.23	2.20
HIGH	2.60	2.80	1.60	4.20	1.57	2.65
M(I) LOW	3.13	3.00	1.60	4.05	1.53	3.40
HIGH	4.60	1.95	2.15	4.40	1.90	4.12

Note: $N = 96$; for abbreviations, see Table 4.10.

The achievement orientations of the members and the climate show significant interaction. Attention is maximum when both are high and it is minimum when the member is high on achievement orientation and the climate is low on it. When the climate nurtures the members' need (achievement), it (climate) is perceived as paying attention. But when the climate itself is low on *n* Ach but the member has high *n* Ach, clearly, the atmosphere is not conducive and it results in less attention.

The achievement orientation of the members and independence orientation of the climate interacted significantly to predict members' attention. Attention is maximum when both these orientations are high and it is minimum when the member is high on achievement orientation but the climate is low on independence orientation. Evidently, independence given by the climate helps the members to satisfy their achievement needs. Thus, a person high on *n* Ach working in an independence-oriented climate perceives more attention.

Finally, the power orientation of the members and achievement orientation of the climate show a significant interaction. Attention is maximum when the member is low on power and the climate is high on achievement orientation. Attention is minimum when both these orientations are low.

Members' Latitude

Five interactions significantly predicted members' perception of latitude. Both beta coefficients and R^2 change are provided in Table 4.12 and the means in Table 4.17.

Table 4.17

Mean Scores—Members' Latitude as a Function of Members' Personal Orientations and Climate Perceptions (Study 2)

MC		MC(P)		MC(A)		MC(I)	
	M	LOW	HIGH	LOW	HIGH	LOW	HIGH
	LOW	2.70	1.60	1.90	3.42	1.90	2.60
M(P)							
	HIGH	2.20	1.70	2.34	2.70	1.60	3.27
	LOW	2.50	1.73	2.60	2.70	2.14	2.20
M(A)							
	HIGH	2.20	2.67	1.80	3.60	1.77	2.55
	LOW	2.33	2.70	1.87	3.25	1.73	2.85
M(I)							
	HIGH	3.50	1.55	3.75	3.40	1.57	3.36

Note: N = 96; for abbreviations, see Table 4.10.

The achievement orientations of both the members and the climate show a significant interaction effect. Latitude was maximum when the members' and the climate's achievement orientations were high and it (latitude) was minimum when the members had a high *n* Ach and the climate showed low *n* Ach. The explanation for this interaction is given in the previous sections.

The achievement orientation of the members also combines with the independence orientation of the climate to predict latitude.

Latitude is maximum when a member is high on achievement need and works in an independence-oriented climate, but it is minimum when the same member (high n Ach) works in a climate which is low on independence orientation. Clearly, independence orientation of the climate has direct implications for latitude. This effect gets more pronounced when combined with the achievement needs of the members.

The independence orientation of the members is also found to combine with power orientation of the climate. Latitude is perceived to be maximum when the member is high on independence and the climate is low on power, and it (latitude) is minimum when the member has high independence needs but the climate, too, is high on power orientation. Obviously, power orientation of the climate thwarts the independence of the members—hence, these results.

The power orientation of the members interacts significantly with the independence orientation of the climate in predicting latitude. Latitude is maximum when the member is high on power need and the climate is high on independence orientation, but the same latitude drops to a minimum when the member is high on power and the climate too is high on independence. Evidently, the independence orientation of the climate helps the members to satisfy their power needs. High independence of the climate facilitates members' need for power but low independence hinders the satisfaction of power needs of the members.

Finally, the achievement orientation of the climate and power orientation of the members show a significant interaction. Latitude is maximum when the member is high on need for power and works in a low n Ach climate. On the other hand, the latitude is minimum when the same member works in a high independence-oriented climate. It seems that achievement orientation of the climate comes in the way of the satisfaction of the members' need for power. How and why elude reasoning.

Thus, LMX, attention, and latitude of the members—all three—were predicted by personal attributes–climate interactions.

Comments

So far, we have been focusing on individual interaction results counting the leaves on the trees. Now, we shall attempt to understand the results more broadly in a comparative framework.

It is evident from the results that person–environment interaction is viable for predicting members' quality of exchange, but the same interaction is not useful for leaders' quality of exchange. As mentioned earlier, the climate is perceived to be partly set by the leaders (Likert, 1967) and can be taken as the leaders' working style. Thus, the quality of interaction from the members' perspective is a function of the *fit* between member's own attributes and the climate as well as style.

Before we proceed with the discussion of significant interaction results, it is worthwhile to state a few points. First, the antecedents—personal attributes and climate—are taken to be relatively fixed and are presumed to be the same at the early stages of role taking in such a way that the earliest evaluations are in terms of these person–environment interactions. Second, these earliest antecedent interactions lead to collaboration on unstructured tasks. Our measures of quality of exchange are the derivatives or outcomes of this collaboration. Thus, perceived contribution, affect, LMX, attention, and latitude are all supposed to be built around this collaboration. Hence, all our interactions in the previous section are discussed in terms of need-press framework to explain collaboration by the members. As a result, the independent aspects of contribution, affect, exchange, attention, and latitude are not discussed in terms of their individual conceptualizations. All the interactions are explained in general for collaboration. This does not mean that these different dimensions do not have independent antecedents. Identification of antecedents at the role-making stage, when active exchanges are dominant, may reveal different dynamics for these dimensions of quality of exchange.

The different measures/dimensions of quality of exchange are similar yet they differ from each other in terms of conceptualization. Of all the five measures—perceived contribution, affect, LMX, attention, and latitude—only affect is relational and affective in nature. All the other four focus on actual working relationships on the job. Thus, if at all, there are any differences in antecedent conditions, they should be for affect. Except for power–power and independence–independence interactions, all others were common to the perceived contribution. Power–power interaction was also significant for LMX. It should be noted that LMX includes one item on satisfaction with the leader and that provides affective component to the scale (Graen & Scandura, 1987). Thus, power and independence orientations of the members and the climate are more salient for affective aspects of the interaction. It, however, has to be pointed out here that these antecedents are for the members' quality of exchange. Members' exercise of power and use of independence in the dyadic interaction, takes special significance, because as members there is little scope for them to satisfy these needs. Consequently, the satisfaction of these needs for the members leads to general satisfaction with and liking for the leaders.

Next, another interaction that needs special mention is between the achievement orientations of the members and the climate. To a limited extent, the n Ach of the members can be taken as a reflection of their competence, and the competence of subordinates has been shown to be an important antecedent factor in predicting LMX (Kim & Organ, 1982; Snyder & Bruning, 1985). The managers' career progress is a function of the initial status in the work-group (IN/OUT) with reference to the leader (Wakabayashi & Graen, 1984) and also of their need for achievement (Andrews, 1967; Hundal, 1971). Theoretically, one can conceive of a sequence wherein n Ach of the members predicts their (members') IN/OUT-Group status which finally leads to career progress. But, the need for achievement of the members needs to get the right kind of working atmosphere (climate) to bloom. Thus, the interaction of achievement orientations of the climate and the members is important in predicting quality of exchange. This interaction was significant for almost all the analyses—perceived contribution (both the studies), affect (both the studies), attention, and latitude. Only LMX could not be predicted by this interaction. No other interaction appeared to be significant with so much of consistency.

Clearly, all the significant interactions for perceived contribution and affect that emerged in both the studies are stronger interactions. In this light, interactions for perceived contribution showed more consistency than affect.

In essence, the person–environment interaction is effective in predicting members' quality of exchange.

Conclusions

In the LMX/VDL theorization, one begins with the assumption of heterogeneity of the work-group, as opposed to the assumption of homogeneity of the ALS theorists. The ALS formulators focused on leader behavior and tried to understand and evaluate its dynamics. In their theorization, subordinates were treated as a work-group. Thus in explaining the phenomenon of leadership, they focused on the variables that related to the leaders themselves (trait or behavior) and/or on other general situational variables (e.g., contingency approaches).

In LMX/VDL, too, the leader behavior is important. But, since the theorization does not begin with the assumption of homogeneity and seeks to unravel the actual dynamics of work-unit functioning, other variables gain importance. As it has been shown amply (see Chapters 1 and 3), unit differentiation does actually occur. It now becomes imperative that the leader behavior be understood and explained in this light. The differentiation of a work-unit is in terms of the subordinates and their interaction with the leader. Since subordinates are individuals (instead of a passive work-group), an evaluation of leadership has to involve the members too. Thus, both the leader- and the member-related variables are important in understanding leadership.

In line with this, at the very first step, we hypothesized that the personal attributes of the leader and the member (in a dyad) should interact in particular ways (e.g., following either the similarity or the complementarity rule) to predict the quality of interaction both for the leaders and for the members. The hypothesis did not find enough support in its favor and the interactions did not predict the quality of interaction—neither for the leader nor for the member. These attributes were general attitudes towards work and we have already discussed the possible causes for the failure of this hypothesis.

Next, we focused on more direct, narrow, and relevant orientations (i.e., orientations towards leadership). Since the interaction is in the context of leadership, the leadership orientations are more immediate and relevant antecedents. Presumably, the interaction of the leaders' and the members' orientations towards leadership yielded significant results. The evaluations are made only from the members' or subordinates perspective. But the interaction should significantly predict leaders' quality of exchange too, though the direction of each interaction might vary.

Finally, a typical person–environment interaction also yields significant results for the members. But the other member of the dyad (i.e., the leader) is seen as instrumental in the creation of the environment (climate). Thus, any identification of equivalent conceptualization of the climate from the leaders' perspective must take this aspect of 'instrumental other' into consideration.

In summary, the study identifies antecedent conditions only for members' quality of exchange (interaction). From the leader perspective, none could be identified. But this should not undermine the importance of the results. If leaders' effectiveness (be all and end all for most theorists) is a function of the members' (workgroup's) performance, evaluation from the members' perspective is equally (if not more) important.

◄ Chapter 5 ►

Behavioral Consequences of the Quality of Interaction

An Overview

No matter what conceptualization of leadership we focus on, and a review of the literature reveals that there are many, each of them recognizes the importance of leadership and its wide-ranging influences. Thus, leadership is a trait that conditions collective responses (Bernard, 1926); it is a behavior of directing and coordinating the activities of the group members (Fiedler, 1967; Hemphill 1949). If leadership is understood as a particular type of power relationship, then the members believe that the leader has the right to influence them and their behavior (Janda, 1960), and so on. The potential and actual influence of leaders or leadership is much recognized and is at the heart of almost all the theorizations. Almost all the theories have incorporated this aspect in their conceptualizations implicitly or explicitly.

In the present chapter, we investigate some of the outcomes of our conceptualization of leadership. As mentioned in Chapter 1, our interest has been in the distal outcomes which are the outcomes of the quality of exchange between a leader and a member. Thus, the present chapter is divided into two parts.

The first part deals with the use of influence tactics by the leaders and the members. The influence tactics used by the two are studied as the outcomes of quality of exchange. After giving the background of social influence in the first section of this part, some hypotheses (conjectures) are stated in the second section. Results are presented and discussed in the third section, followed by some comments in the final one.

In the second part, some other outcomes for the members are discussed. In the first section of this part, the outcomes of satisfaction, commitment, intent to leave, and unit effectiveness are reviewed in the context of leadership. Based on this and on our review of literature on LMX/VDL in Chapter 1, some hypotheses (conjectures) are presented in the second section of the same part. Results and discussion of the survey data are presented in the third section. Finally, some comments on the results are made in the fourth section.

Social Influence

The Background

Power is an important and pervasive phenomenon in organizations and has been studied at every conceivable level—between different organizations (e.g., Kochan, 1975), within an organization between different subunits (e.g., Salancik & Pfeffer, 1974), and among organizational members (e.g., Ansari, 1990; Bachman, Bowers, & Marcus, 1968; Kipnis et al., 1980; Patchen, 1974).

Power is an elementary and fundamental concept in social sciences just as 'energy is the fundamental concept in physics' (Russell, 1938, p. 18). Since it is a fundamental concept, it has been understood in different frameworks. In the Lewinian *field* approach, it is the force (resultant) that *A* uses to influence some region of *B*'s lifespace (Cartwright, 1959).

March (1955) understands power in the context of *decision-making*. According to him, power or influence is to be understood in terms of inducement of change in an organization. Thus, influence is studied and ascertained by determining its consequences. In this framework, Dahl (1957) explains *A*'s power over *B* as follows: It is the probability that *B* will behave in a particular way after *A* intervenes (exerts power) as against the probability of *B* indulging in that behavior without *A*'s intervention.

Thibaut and Kelley (1959) conceptualize power in an *interaction* framework of outcomes in exchanges. According to them, *A*'s power over *B* is *A*'s ability to affect the quality of *B*'s outcomes. The extent of *A*'s power is a direct function of the range of *B*'s experienced outcomes. Besides these three major frameworks, power has been understood as a latent force (Bierstedt, 1950) and, as a personality construct (Minton, 1967).

These are the broad categories for understanding the concept of power in general. For present purposes, power needs to be understood to explain and understand influence processes in organizations. We will take up power again later in connection with leadership processes but for now let us focus on power and influence.

Power and Influence

Power, as stated earlier, has been defined through a wide-ranging array of concepts. It is because power is a fundamental concept and is multifaceted that the researchers have focused on different aspects of power depending upon their aims and requirements. Thus, some have focused on *sources* of power (e.g., French & Raven, 1959); others have understood it as social control (Dahl, 1957); still others (e.g., Khandwalla, 1977) have viewed it as a *general capacity* of individuals.

Researchers have been interested in making a distinction between potential and realized power. This aspect focuses on the possession of power as being distinct from its (power's) actual use. Potential power is realized only when there is an observable attempt to influence (Wrong, 1968). This distinction between potential and enacted components of power has also been identified by the exchange theorists (Blau, 1964; Emerson, 1962). Minton (1967) calls the two as latent (potential) and manifest (realized) powers and gives a more detailed description of the two. According to him, elements of effectiveness, influence, and attempts to gain power exemplify manifest power, whereas only expressed feelings of and readiness to apply power represent latent power.

Essentially, power and influence are not synonymous (e.g., Dahl, 1957; Katz & Kahn, 1978). Power is the ability to influence, it does not need to be enacted but influence has to be. Influence, hence, is the manifested (demonstrated) use of power such that, it (influence) brings out some behavioral and psychological effects in the target person.

We see that though power and influence are taken as two distinct concepts, there are close links between the two. Thus, if one were to see how some people are more influential than others, bases of power will be the best place to start with, because bases of power are the actual sources of influence.

Sources of Influence

A base of power is the source of influence in a social relationship. Different researchers have identified different bases of power in different frameworks. Etzioni (1975) identified three types of power—coercive, remunerative, and normative—with three parallel types of involvement, viz., alienative, calculative, and emotional, on the part of organizational participants. Peabody (1962) also enumerated three sources of power: position, competence, and personal. Reviews (e.g., Yukl, 1981) of the literature in this area suggest that, of all the classificatory schemes, French and Raven's (1959) seems to be the most widely used and studied taxonomy. In their original (1959) classification, they identified five bases of power—reward, coercive, legitimate, referent, and expert. Subsequently, two more—information and connection—were added to the original list (Hersey, Blanchard, & Natemeyer, 1979; Raven, 1965). Before dealing with the effects of the use of different bases of power, an understanding of these bases is in order:

A is said to have *reward* power over B, if B perceives that A has the capacity to give out rewards. A will have *coercive* power, if B perceives that A can either eliminate rewards or can administer punishments. If B perceives that A has got the right to influence and B is obliged to get influenced, then A has *legitimate* power over B. A will have *referent* power over B, if B perceives A to be attractive. The attraction could be based on friendship, identification with a successful model, and the like. If B perceives A as having technical knowledge and expertise then, A has *expert* power over B. Similarly, if B perceives that A has some valuable and rare information, then *A* has *information* power over *B*. Finally, if *A* is perceived to have connection and links with other influential people (inside or outside the organization), *A* has *connection* power over *B*.

For a manager, use of one source of power may have implications for his or her other bases of power. For example, if a leader doles out rewards, he or she is liked much by the members, thus leading to an increase in his/her referent power. Thus, the study of one base of power in isolation is meaningless, as a host of them could be operating together at one time. Just as one base of power gets enhanced (referent) by the use of another (reward), the use of one base also has the potential to negate others. For example, use of coercion may lead to public acceptance of the influence attempt but privately the influence agent may be disliked outrageously (Raven & Kruglanski, 1970), thus leading to a decrease in referent power.

Yukl (1981) while summarizing the findings on bases of power, points out that generally referent and expert bases of power have positive relationships with satisfaction, and negative correlation with absenteeism and turnover. Legitimate and coercive powers are either unrelated or negatively related with positive criterion measures; use of reward power shows no clear trend. After summarizing the studies on power bases, Yukl (1981) recommends that, besides studying power bases, power research can also provide information about the actual use of influence attempts by the managers. Thus, what we are interested in is the behavioral manifestation of these power bases. These behavioral manifestations are called 'influence strategies.'

Influence Strategies

Goodchilds, Quadrado, and Raven (1975) started the identification of influence strategies by directly asking the subjects, either orally or through written essays, questions about the strategies they used to influence others. The introduction of this methodology gave impetus to research on influence strategies. A number of influence strategies have been identified (e.g., Goodchilds et al., 1975; Kipnis, 1976; Kipnis et al., 1980). It needs to be mentioned here that though some of the influence strategies fall into the power bases given by French and Raven (1959) and other frameworks, not all of them do. For example, use of coalition, ingratiation, etc., do not fall into the French and Raven classification. Thus, a description of power bases is not sufficient to study influence strategies used in organizational settings.

Further, researchers have employed Goodchilds et al.'s (1975) procedure to identify influence strategies in varying contexts (e.g., Ansari, Kapoor, & Rehana, 1984; Falbo, 1977, 1982; Falbo & Peplau, 1980; Goodstein, 1981). Influence strategies to influence friends and parents by the students (Goodchilds et al., 1975), lovers and spouses (Kipnis, 1976; Kipnis, Cohn, & Schwarz, 1976), bosses, coworkers, and subordinates (e.g., Ansari et al., 1984; Kipnis et al., 1980) have been tapped. Influence strategies used in different contexts show a lot of overlap. Following is a brief description of influence strategies used for upward (bosses), downward (subordinates), and lateral (co-workers) influence in organizations.

Assertiveness or Assertion, involves forcefully telling and demanding, showing verbal anger, pointing out rules, etc. (Kipnis, 1976). *Coalition* uses pressure by getting the support of coworkers and subordinates. Coalition is more often used for upward influence. As is obvious from the name, *exchange of benefits* involves exchange of favors and personal sacrifices. *Ingratiation* contains the elements of making the other person feel important, flattery, praise, etc. *Manipulation* involves influencing others, with the target person being unaware of being influenced (Mowday, 1978; Porter, Allen, & Angle, 1981). This too, like coalition, is used more frequently for upward influence. According to Allen, Madison, Porter, Renwick, and Mayes (1979), manipulation involves withholding or distorting information to influence. *Reasoning* involves the use of rational methods like giving reasons, explaining, writing memos and detailed plans, and providing facts and data to influence. *Defiance* or *threat* is used when negative consequences (for the failure of influence attempt) are stated. *Upward appeal* involves bringing pressure from someone higher up in the organizational hierarchy. Finally, the *use of sanctions* draws upon rewards and punishments in organizations. It involves both informal (e.g., praising or criticizing) and formal (e.g., promotion or demotion) exchanges (Kipnis

& Vanderveer, 1971; Mechanic, 1962; Porter et al., 1981). Another tactic which has been found more relevant in the Indian setting involves helping the target in personal matters and is called *personalized help*.

These are some of the most common strategies used in organizations. Different researchers have provided different frameworks to understand and explicate these strategies. According to Wilkinson and Kipnis (1978), these strategies can either be weak or strong. Withholding payments, threats, etc. are strong strategies; request for compliance and compromise are considered to be weak strategies. In the same vein, Falbo (1977) identified two dimensions—rational/nonrational and direct/indirect—in which influence strategies could be placed. Reasoning, compromise, etc. are rational tactics; deciet, evasion, etc. are nonrational. For the second dimension, strategies of like assertion, etc. are direct and manipulation, etc. are the indirect methods. Later, in the context of intimate relations, Falbo (1982) gave a two-dimensional framework to understand power strategies. One dimension consisted of the directness (direct to indirect) and the other of the interactiveness (bilateral to unilateral) of the strategies. Similarly, Farrell and Peterson (1982) identified three dimensions in the context of political behavior: internal-external, vertical-lateral, and legitimate-illegitimate. A wide range of strategies are mapped in these three dimensions: for example, whistle blowing, lawsuits (external and illegitimate); exchange of favors, trading agreements, etc. (internal and legitimate); bypassing the chain of command, etc. (vertical); offering help, coalition, etc. (lateral).

Thus, besides identifying different influence strategies, researchers have also identified broad frameworks and models to understand and explain them. Further, attempts have been made to see the position of influence strategies vis-à-vis other relevant variables like need for power (Kapoor, 1987; McClelland, 1975), self-confidence (Falbo, 1977; Raven & Kruglanski, 1970), cognitions of the power-holder (Kipnis, 1976), goals of influence attempts (Ansari & Kapoor, 1987; Kipnis & Schmidt, 1983), attribution of success and failure on influence strategies (Schilit & Locke, 1982; Tandon, Ansari, & Kapoor, 1989). Leadership is another such variable that needs to be studied along with power and influence.

Leadership and Bases of Power

The obvious and very direct link between power and leadership can be understood in Cartwright's (1965) conceptualization of influence. According to him when an agent (exerting influence) O performs an act resulting in some change in another agent (subjected to influence) P, we say that O influences P. Extending this concept of influence, Kochan, Schmidt, and de Cotiis (1975, p. 285) define leadership in that framework (see Chapter 1 for the definition). Thus, influence is common to both—leadership and power.

So far as research on leadership and power is concerned, the major thrust of the researchers has been on the relationship between power bases and leader behavior. Kipnis (1958), in one of the earliest attempts, compared the effectiveness of directive and participative leadership styles in conjunction with reward and punishment. The effectiveness was measured in terms of public compliance and private acceptance (by the members) of the influence attempt. The results showed that though public compliance was same for all the conditions, private acceptance showed some interesting variations. Participative leadership showed more private acceptance than directive leadership for the reward condition, but less private acceptance for the punishment condition. Mulder and his associates (Mulder, de Jong, Koppelaar, & Verhage, 1977) investigated the relationship between power and leadership in a banking concern. They found that the leaders exerted more formal, referent, and expert powers in crisis situations than in noncrisis situations. Further, they found that the crisis/noncrisis nature of the situation moderated the relationship between the type of leadership and the effectiveness of the leader. Subsequently, Mulder, Binkhorst, and Van Oers (1983) suggested that, in crisis situations (difficult requirements), consultants should be able to exert power forcefully and should be able to maintain open relationships with others. Martin and Hunt (1980), in a systematic, path-analytic study, were mainly concerned with investigating the effect of social influence on intent to leave. Their study also revealed how the use of different bases of power resulted in the difference in the perception of the leaders' behavior. These results showed variations across different units (bureaus).

Leadership and Influence Strategies

Studies relating leadership with influence strategies are few and far between. Most of them have been concerned with evaluating leaders' use of strategies to influence subordinates and their effect on them (subordinates).

Kipnis, Schmidt, Price, and Stitt (1981) examined the effect of leaders' use of influence strategies on their assessment of the followers' motives via employee evaluations. Their results revealed that the leaders who were expected to act democratically showed a greater use of noncontrolling influence strategies and those expected to act autocratically showed a greater use of controlling influence strategies. Further, leaders using controlling tactics reported that their subordinates were not self-motivated and those using noncontrolling tactics attributed the subordinate performance to their self-motivation. In yet another study, C.B.P. Singh (1985) investigated the effect of leadership styles on their influence strategies. He reported that four styles—people-orientation, power orientation, impersonal orientation, and suspicion and limited role—predicted the use of different influence strategies. For example, the suspicion and limited role style predicted the use of strategies like reliance, psuedo-nurturance, and diplomacy.

The discussion, so far, leads us to the conclusion that it is only the leaders who influence and use different strategies to influence the subordinates. This is not really the case. Although the mutuality of influence processes has been recognized, few studies have investigated this aspect. All the same, there have been efforts to identify the influence of the subordinates over their leaders in different contexts (e.g., Grosser, Polansky, & Lippitt, 1951; Polansky, Lippitt, & Redl, 1950). A direct test of the two-way influence process has been provided by Bass (1975) in a simulation (field experimental) setting, by Herold (1977) in an experimental setting, and by Greene (1979) in a survey research.

Though the fact about mutual influence processes has been recognized, there have been very few studies (e.g. Ansari, 1990) evaluating the actual use of strategies used by the subordinates.

Based on these deficiencies and needs, we now frame our hypotheses in the present micro-level analysis.

Some Conjectures

In our dyadic framework each party makes demands on the other. Each one's job is defined and decided through negotiations.

In this work, we focus on both the upward (used by the members) and the downward (used by the leaders) influence strategies. Also, we investigate whether it is the average or individual quality of interaction that predicts the use of different strategies. Dienesch and Liden (1986) also presume (theoretically) an interaction effect of the quality of interaction dimension on certain outcome variables. Hence, the following hypothesis are proposed

H5.1: Leaders' influence strategies (downward) are a function of their quality of interaction (perceived contribution and affect).

H5.2: Leaders' influence strategies are a function of the interaction of their perceived contribution and affect.

H5.3: Members' influence strategies (upward) are a function of their own quality of interaction.

H5.4: Members' influence strategies are a function of the interaction of their perceived contribution and affect.

H5.5: Members' influence strategies are better predicted by their individual (VDL) as compared to the average (ALS) quality of exchange.

It needs to be mentioned here that even the leader's use of influence strategy is expected to be predicted better by the individual (VDL) quality of interaction than by the group scores. But this contention could not be tested here because of the lack of sufficient data.

Specifically, rational (e.g., reasoning) and informal and weak strategies (e.g., personalized exchange) are expected to be a direct function of the quality of interaction. Formal and strong strategies (e.g., assertion) are expected to be inversely related to the quality of interaction from both the perspectives.

Results and Discussion

Downward Influence Strategies

As a test of our first hypothesis (H5.1) both the quality of interaction measures—perceived contribution and affect—were put in a stepwise regression equation as predictors for each of the seven influence strategies. This hypothesis was tested only in Study 1. Zero-order correlations between the predictors and criterion variables are reported in Table 5.1. The regression results for hypothesis 1 are given in Table 5.2.

Table 5.1

Zero-order Correlations between Leaders' Quality of Interaction (Predictors) and Influence Tactics (Criterion Variables) (Study 1)

	IES	I	PE	R	PR	A	SE
PC	−.35	−.13	.36	.34	−.48	−.53	−.19
AF	.13	.28	−.15	.21	−.30	−.32	−.11

Note: $r (150) = .21$ at $p < .01$; $r (150) = .16$ at $p < .05$; IES = Informal External Support; I = Ingratiation; PE = Personalized Exchange; R = Reasoning; PR = Persuasion; A = Assertion; SE = Showing Expertise; PC = Perceived Contribution; AF = Affect.

It can be seen that perceived contribution, in general, is a better predictor of influence strategies than affect. It significantly predicts the use of informal external support, personalized exchange, reasoning, persuasion, and assertion. Affect predicts the use of assertion. However, the use of showing expertise as a strategy could not be predicted significantly by any of the two quality of interaction dimensions.

It is evident from the tables that both, personalized exchange and reasoning, are a direct function of perceived contribution. On the other hand, informal external support, persuasion, and assertion are a negative function of the same. The results are much in line with our conjectures.

Reasoning is a rational tactic and hence its use for the subordinates with high perceived contribution seems justified. Further, since better quality dyads are characterized with informal exchanges, the use of personalized exchanges, too, is much in consonance with our argument. The leader uses more of informal external support, persuasion, and assertion, if their perceived contribution is low. Clearly, the leader uses formal and strong measures to influence these subordinates (i.e., lower quality of interaction). Earlier work by Ansari, Tandon, and Lakhtakia (1989) reported similar results.

Table 5.2
Stepwise Regression Results—Leaders' Quality of Interaction
(Predictors) and Leaders' Influence Strategies (Criterion Variables)
(Study 1)

Predictors	Criterion	PC	AF
IES			
	R	.35	*
	R² change	.12	*
	Beta	−.35[a]	*
	Order	1	*
I			
	R	.29	.28
	R² change	.00	.08
	Beta	−.03	.30[a]
	Order	2	1
PE			
	R	.36	.36
	R² change	.13	.00
	Beta	.38[a]	−.05
	Order	1	2
R			
	R	.34	.34
	R² change	.11	.00
	Beta	.31[a]	.04
	Order	1	2
PR			
	R	.48	.48
	R² change	.23	.00
	Beta	−.44[a]	−.07
	Order	1	2
A			
	R	.53	.48
	R² change	28	.00
	Beta	−.50[a]	−.06
	Order	1	2
SE			
	R	.19	.19
	R² change	.03	.00
	Beta	−.18	−.02
	Order	1	2

Note: $N = 152$; $a = p < .01$; * Tolerance level insufficient for further computations; IES = Informal External Support; I = Ingratiation; PE = Personalized Exchange, R = Reasoning; PR = Persuasion, A = Assertion; SE = Showing Pertise; PC = Perceived Contribution; AF = Affect.

Thus, clearly, the leaders' use of different strategies to influence the subordinates is determined by their (leaders') quality of exchange with their members.

The interaction of the two dimensions (perceived contribution and affect) of the quality of interaction predicted the use of only one strategy—Informal External Support. The hierarchical regression results are reported in Table 5.3 and the means are reported in Table 5.4. Leaders used the strategy of informal external support the most when both, perceived contribution and affect, were low; the use of this strategy was minimum when perceived contribution was high but affect was low. Thus, a combination of low quality of interaction leads to a greater use of informal external support. Except this influence strategy, no other strategy could be predicted

Table 5.3

Hierarchical Regression Results—Interaction of the Leaders' Perceived Contribution and Affect as a Determinant of Their Influence Strategies (Study 1)

	PC	$(-.16^a, .12)$
IES	AF	$(-.06, .00)$
	PC × AF	$(.33^a, .09)$
	PC	$(.05, .02)$
I	AF	$(.27^a, .06)$
	PC × AF	$(.13, .01)$
	PC	$(.35^a, .13)$
PE	AF	$(-.04, .00)$
	PC × AF	$(-.06, .00)$
	PC	$(.24^a, .11)$
R	AF	$(.07, .01)$
	PC × AF	$(-.13, .01)$
	PC	$(-.43^a, .23)$
PR	AF	$(-.08, .00)$
	PC × AF	$(.02, .00)$
	PC	$(-.51^a, .28)$
A	AF	$(-.06, .00)$
	PC × AF	$(-.01, .00)$
	PC	$(-.15^b, .03)$
SE	AF	$(-.03, .00)$
	PC × AF	$(.05, .00)$

Note: $N = 152$; a $p < .01$; IES = Informal External Support; I = Ingratiation; PE = Personalized Exchange; R = Reasoning; PR = Persuasion; A = Assertion; SE = Showing Expertise; PC = Perceived Contribution; AF = Affect. Figures in parantheses indicate beta coefficients and R^2 change, respectively.

Table 5.4

Mean Scores—Leaders' Influence Strategies as a Function of the
Interaction of Their Perceived Contribution and Affect (Study 1)

	PC		
	AF	Low	High
IES	Low	15.64	13.21
	High	14.65	15.41
I	Low	15.99	16.36
	High	19.29	21.91
PE	Low	17.36	25.00
	High	19.23	18.36
R	Low	20.39	20.86
	High	20.71	21.36
PR	Low	11.14	09.50
	High	10.29	08.09
A	Low	08.45	06.79
	High	08.53	06.27
SE	Low	27.18	26.07
	High	25.00	25.00

Note: See Table 5.3.

by this interaction. In general, hence, the interaction hypothesis does not find enough support. Though the two dimensions independently do predict the use of influence strategies, jointly they do not.

Next, we focus on the members' use of influence strategies.

Upward Influence Strategies

The next three hypotheses (H5.3, H5.4, and H5.5) are concerned with the members' use of strategies to influence their leaders. Three main predictors are taken up—the independent effects of the quality of exchange, joint effect of the two dimensions of the quality of interaction, and a comparison of average and individual measures of the quality of exchange.

Independent Effects of Quality of Exchange

Hypothesis 3 was tested in Study 1 and then retested in Study 2. In Study 1, three quality of exchange measures—perceived contribution, affect, and leader–member exchanges (LMX)—were taken as the predictors of different influence strategies used by the members. In Study 2, four quality of exchange measures—perceived contribution, affect, attention, and latitude—were taken as the predictors. The results of Study 1 and then Study 2 are discussed in the following sections.

Study 1 Results

The zero-order correlations between the three predictors and five criterion variables are reported in Table 5.5. The results of stepwise regression analysis are reported in Table 5.6.

Table 5.5

Zero-order Correlations of the Members' Quality of Exchange (Predictors) with Their Influence Strategies and Other Outcome Variables (Study 1)

	IN					OUT			
	IES	*I*	*PE*	*R*	*PR*	*ES*	*IS*	*CO*	*IL*
PC	−.09	.21	.26	.31	.03	.34	.35	.35	−.18
AF	.07	−.29	.27	.11	.10	.28	.26	.27	−.17
LMX	−.06	.19	.21	.39	.02	.33	.38	.38	−.15

Note: r (150) = .21 at $p < .01$; r (150) = .16; at $p < .05$; IN = Influence Strategies; IES = Informal External Support; I = Ingratiation; PE = Personalized Exchange; R = Reasoning; PR = Persuasion; ES = Extrinsic Satisfaction; IS = Intrinsic Satisfaction; CO = Commitment; IL = Intent to Leave; PC = Perceived Contribution; AF = Affect; LMX = Leader-Member Exchanges; OUT = Other Outcome Variables.

The use of informal external support could not be predicted significantly by any of the three quality of exchange measures. Ingratiation is best predicted by affect. Seemingly, members ingratiate when the affect is low for the leaders. This means that all the positive words and praises the member uses are mere verbal tactics to get his or her way. Ingratiation is not considered a rational tactic; it is more a part of politiking and manipulation. The use of this strategy by the members who have little affect for the leader reinforces this contention.

Personalized exchange, too, is predicted best by affect. Unlike ingratiation, personalized exchange is used more when affect for

Table 5.6
Stepwise Regression Results—Members' Quality of Exchange
(Predictors) and Their Influence Strategies (Study 1)

Predictors	Criterion	PC	AF	LMX
IES				
	R	.09	.17	.17
	R^2 change	.01	.02	.00
	Beta	− .15	.17	− .03
	Order	1	2	3
I				
	R	.30	.29	.30
	R^2 change	.00	.08	.00
	Beta	.10	− .25[b]	− .01
	Order	2	1	3
PE				
	R	.30	.27	.30
	R^2 change	.02	.06	.00
	Beta	.19	.19[b]	− .04
	Order	2	1	3
R				
	R	.44	.44	.39
	R^2 change	.00	.04	.15
	Beta	.06	.19[b]	.43[a]
	Order	3	2	1
PR				
	R	*	.10	.10
	R^2 change	*	.01	.00
	Beta	*	.01	.00
	Order	*	1	2

Note: $N = 152$; a $p < .01$; b $p < .05$; * tolerance level insufficient for further computations. For abbreviations, see Table 5.5.

the leader is high. Essentially, more affect means more interaction with the leader and a greater willingness to help the leader on personal aspects. This shows that whereas the use of personalized exchange is genuine, ingratiation is not.

Reasoning was best predicted by LMX followed by affect. In line with our conceptualization of dyadic interactions, reasoning should be used for influence on the actual job situation. Therefore, it (reasoning) should be better predicted by the quality of exchange measures containing elements of actual job situations. The LMX is essentially work oriented and if it predicts the use of reasoning, it seems justified. All the same, members' affect for their leader too predicts the use of reasoning. Obviously, members give reasons when they have a high affect for him or her (the leader).

Finally, the use of persuasion could not be predicted by any of the three quality of exchange measures.

It is interesting to note that though for the leaders perceived contribution was a better predictor, for the members affect was a better predictor. Moreover, whereas the predictive strength is high for the leaders' perspective, it is usually not so strong for the members' perspective. We will take up these observations a little later (see section on comments). For the moment, let us look at the Study 2 results.

Study 2 Results

Zero-order correlations between the four predictors—perceived contribution, affect, attention, and latitude (individual scores)—and five influence strategies (criterion measures) are give in Table 5.7. Results of the stepwise regression analysis are reported in Table 5.8.

Table 5.7

Zero-order Correlations of the Members' Quality of Exchange (Individual and Group Scores as Predictors) with Their Influence Strategies and Other Outcome Variables (Study 2)

		IN					OUT			
		IES	I	PE	R	PR	ES	IS	CO	UE
PC	Id	−.58	−.08	.21	.58	−.25	.57	.50	.59	.60
	Gr	−.14	.01	−.10	.23	−.24	.40	.33	.31	.11
AF	Id	−.51	.01	.21	.49	−.16	.49	.52	.57	.62
	Gr	−.17	.14	.08	.24	−.03	.40	.38	.34	.28
AT	Id	−.66	−.06	.34	.66	−.19	.58	.47	.66	.74
	Gr	−.17	−.05	.12	.24	.02	.35	.22	.27	.25
LT	Id	−.63	−.10	.32	.60	−.19	.55	.42	.60	.70
	Gr	−.19	−.09	.02	.14	−.02	.23	.13	.24	.23

Note: r (94) = .19 at p < .01; r (94) = .26 at p < .05; IN = Influence Strategies; OUT = Other Outcome Variables, IES = Informal External Support; I = Ingratiation; PE = Personalized Exchange; R = Reasoning; PR = Persuasion; ES = Extrinsic Satisfaction; IS = Intrinsic Satisfaction; CO = Commitment; UE = Unit Effectiveness; PC = Perceived Contribution; Gr = Group Score; Id = Individual Score.

Table 5.8
Stepwise Regression Results—Members' Quality of Exchange
(Predictors) and Their Influence Strategies (Criterion Variables)
(Study 2)

Predictors					
	Criterion	PC	AF	AT	LT
ISE					
	R	*	*	.66	.69
	R^2 change	*	*	.44	.04
	Beta	*	*	−.43[a]	−.27[b]
	Order	*	*	1	2
I					
	R	*	*	*	*
	R^2 change	*	*	*	*
	Beta	*	*	*	*
	Order	*	*	*	*
PE					
	R	*	*	.34	*
	R^2 change	*	*	.11	*
	Beta	*	*	.34[a]	*
	Order	*	*	1	*
R					
	R	*	*	.66	*
	R^2 change	*	*	.44	*
	Beta	*	*	.66[a]	*
	Order	*	*	1	*
PR					
	R	.25	*	*	*
	R^2 change	.06	*	*	*
	Beta	−.25[b]	*	*	*
	Order	1	*	*	*

Note: $N = 96$; a $p < .01$; b $p < .05$; * Tolerance level insufficient for further computations. For abbreviations, see Table 5.7.

Clearly, attention is the best predictor, predicting three (informal external support, personalized exchange, and persuasion), out of five influence strategies. Use of informal external support is a negative function of attention and latitude. Neither ingratiation nor persuasion could be predicted by any of the four predictors. Personalized exchange and reasoning both are a positive function of attention. If attention is low, the member is likely to go to others (co-workers) for help, but if the attention is high the member indulges in personal exchanges and use of logic to influence the leader.

Surprisingly, affect, unlike in Study 1, did not predict the use of any strategy. However, perceived contribution predicted the use of persuasion. Persuasion was used more by the members when their perceived contribution was low. The member uses pressure tactics (Ansari et al., 1989; Yukl & Falbe, 1990) to influence the leader who is perceived to contribute less.

In Study 1, the best predictor was affect; but in Study 2, attention emerged as the best predictor. Affect did not emerge at all as a predictor of any strategies in Study 2. In Study 1, all the three measures of quality of exchange are the general measures of exchange (e.g., leaders' contribution on the jobs, nature of exchanges, and affect for the leader). Of these three general measures, affect is the best predictor. When these general measures are put along with more specific dimensions (e.g., attention and latitude), the specific dimensions emerge as better predictors of influence strategies. Influence strategies, too, are actual behaviors on the job and their prediction by actual leader behavior (attention) seems justified.

If we look at the global quality of exchange as a predictor of members' influence strategies, personalized exchange and reasoning are a direct function of the quality of exchange (affect and LMX in Study 1, and attention in Study 2)—this is all we have for the consistency of results in both the studies.

In Study 2, the use of informal external support (IES) and persuasion (PR) were also predicted by the quality of exchange measures (unlike in Study 1). Informal external support was an inverse function of both attention and latitude, and like in Study 1, neither perceived contribution nor affect predicted the use of this strategy. But the use of persuasion was predicted by perceived contribution in Study 2 which was not evident in Study 1. This is a discrepancy in the results of the two studies which is difficult to explain.

Interaction Effect of Perceived Contribution and Affect

The interaction effects of the two dimensions of the quality of interaction were evaluated through a hierarchical multiple regression analysis. The regression results are reported in Table 5.9, and the means are reported in Table 5.10.

Table 5.9
Hierarchical Regression Results—Interaction of the Members'
Perceived Contribution and Affect as a Determinant of Their Influence
Strategies (Study 1)

	PC	(−.02, .01)
IES	AF	(.10, .02)
	PC × AF	(.28[a], .06)
	PC	(.17[a], .04)
I	AF	(.21[a], .04)
	PC × AF	(.15, .02)
	PC	(.20[a], .07)
PE	AF	(.17[b], .02)
	PC × AF	(.06, .00)
	PC	(.32[a], .10)
R	AF	(−.06, .00)
	PC × AF	(−.05, .00)
	PC	(−.02, .00)
PR	AF	(.11, .01)
	PC × AF	(.02, .00)

Note: Same as Table 5.3.

Table 5.10
Mean Scores—Members' Influence Strategies as a Function of the
Interaction of Their Perceived Contribution and Affect (Study 1)

	PC AF	Low	High
IES	Low	23.00	16.06
	High	15.00	15.46
I	Low	17.33	16.61
	High	20.17	26.50
PE	Low	15.17	20.15
	High	18.06	23.83
R	Low	20.61	23.69
	High	19.89	22.50
PR	Low	9.63	10.08
	High	9.94	12.83

Note: Same as Table 5.3.

Only IES was predicted by the interaction of perceived contribution (PC) and affect (AF) (Table 5.9). Members used IES the most when both, perceived contribution of and affect for the leader, were low. But it was used the least when the perceived contribution was low and affect was high. Low PC and low AF together make for a poor quality of interaction, which is not a conducive situation for the member to approach the leader directly for any influence attempts. The use of external support to pressurize the leader, in this case, seems appropriate. On the other hand, even if PC is low but AF is high, the member does not depend on the use of external support.

The rest of the four strategies could not be predicted by the interaction of PC and AF. The interaction effects from the members' perspective have a striking similarity to the effects from the leaders' perspective.

In general, thus, the interaction of PC and AF does not significantly predict the use of upward influence strategies. Thus, hypothesis 4 (H5.4) finds little support.

Average vs Individual Quality of Exchange as Predictors

In the last two subsections, we focused on the independent and interaction effects of quality of exchange (QEx) measures. Though main effects were significant, interaction effects were not. Next, we evaluate the relative strengths of *average* and *dyadic* conceptualizations. For this purpose, we take the group quality of exchange representing average QEx and individual QEx representing a differentiated-unit conceptualization.

To evaluate the two together, they were put to a stepwise regression analysis (see Chapter 3). As was mentioned earlier, data from Study 2 (members' perspective) was used for this purpose. The stepwise regression results for PC, AF, AT, and LT are reported in Tables 5.11, 5.12, 5.13, and 5.14, respectively. We shall present each result separately.

The individual scores of perceived contribution predict the use of informal external support, personalized exchange, reasoning, and persuasion at the first step (Table 5.11). Group scores predict the use of personalized exchange (PE) *but* only at the second step. Clearly, individual scores are better predictors. Besides PE, none of the other influence strategies could be predicted by the group scores. Ingratiation could not be predicted by any of the two scores.

Table 5.11
Stepwise Regression Results—Members' Perceived Contribution
(Group and Individual Scores as Predictors) and Their Influence
Strategies (Criterion Variables) (Study 2)

Predictors	Criterion	PC(Id)	PC(Gr)
IES			
	R	.58	*
	R^2 change	.33	*
	Beta	−.58[a]	*
	Order	1	*
I			
	R	*	*
	R^2 change	*	*
	Beta	*	*
	Order	*	*
PE			
	R	.21	.30
	R^2 change	.05	.05
	Beta	.32[a]	−.24[b]
	Order	1	2
R			
	R	.58	*
	R^2 change	.34	*
	Beta	.58[a]	*
	Order	1	*
PR			
	R	.25	*
	R^2 change	.06	*
	Beta	−.25[a]	*
	Order	1	*

Note: $N = 96$; a $p < .01$; b $p < .05$; * Tolerance level insufficient for further computations. For abbreviations, see Table 5.7.

So far as PC is concerned, results for persuasion are of prime importance, as PC (in Study 2) significantly predicts the use of this strategy. It is the individual PC score that predicts the use of this strategy, which is an evidence for variations within a work-group, so far as influencing a leader (with respect to PC) is concerned. Use of personalized exchange is predicted both by the individual and group scores of PC for which there is evidence of both average and dyadic leadership. This is an equivocal (reject) condition and the level of analysis for this cannot be predicted.

Table 5.12

Stepwise Regression Results—Members' Affect (Group and Individual Scores as Predictors) and Their Influence Strategies (Criterion Variables) (Study 2)

Predictors	Criterion	AF(Id)	AF(Gr)
IES			
	R	.51	*
	R^2 change	.26	*
	Beta	−.51[a]	*
	Order	1	*
I			
	R	*	*
	R^2 change	*	*
	Beta	*	*
	Order	*	*
PE			
	R	.21	*
	R^2 change	.04	*
	Beta	.21[b]	*
	Order	1	*
R			
	R	.49	*
	R^2 change	.24	*
	Beta	.49[a]	*
	Order	1	*
PR			
	R	*	*
	R^2 change	*	*
	Beta	*	*
	Order	*	*

Note: $N = 96$; a $p < .01$; b $p < .05$; * Tolerance level insufficient for further computations. For abbreviations, see Table 5.7.

Next, the individual scores of affect predict the use of informal external support, personalized exchange, and reasoning (Table 5.12). The group scores do not predict any influence strategy. Though affect, when put together with other measures of quality of exchange, does not emerge as a significant predictor (Study 2); but when individual and group scores are taken, individual scores are clearly better predictors. This is a direct evidence for dyadic (unit-differentiation) conceptualization.

Table 5.13
Stepwise Regression Results—Members' Attention (Group and Individual Scores as Predictors) and Their Influence Strategies (Criterion Variables) (Study 2)

Predictors	Criterion	AT(Id)	AT(Gr)
IES			
	R	.66	*
	R² change	.43	*
	Beta	− .66ᵃ	*
	Order	1	*
I			
	R	*	*
	R² change	*	*
	Beta	*	*
	Order	*	*
PE			
	R	.34	*
	R² change	.11	*
	Beta	.34ᵃ	*
	Order	1	*
R			
	R	.66	*
	R² change	.44	*
	Beta	.66ᵃ	*
	Order	1	*
PR			
	R	*	*
	R² change	*	*
	Beta	*	*
	Order	*	*

*Note: N = 96; a p < .01; b p < .05; * Tolerance level insufficient for further computations. For abbreviations, see Table 5.7.*

Attention emerged as the best predictor of informal external support, personalized exchange, and reasoning when put along with the other measures of QEx (Table 5.8). For all the three strategies, individual scores of attention are better predictors than the group scores (Table 5.13). Clearly, the individual attention given to the subordinates is a better predictor than collective attention (group AT).

Table 5.14
Stepwise Regression Results—Members' Latitude (Group and Individual Scores as Predictors) and Their Influence Strategies (Criterion Variables) (Study 2)

Predictors	Criterion	LT(Id)	LT(Gr)
IES			
	R	.63	*
	R^2 change	.39	*
	Beta	− .63[a]	*
	Order	1	*
I			
	R	*	*
	R^2 change	*	*
	Beta	*	*
	Order	*	*
PE			
	R	.32	*
	R^2 change	.10	*
	Beta	.32[a]	*
	Order	1	*
R			
	R	.61	*
	R^2 change	.36	*
	Beta	.61[a]	*
	Order	1	*
PR			
	R	*	*
	R^2 change	*	*
	Beta	*	*
	Order	*	*

Note: $N = 96$; a $p < .01$; b $p < .05$; * Tolerance level insufficient for further computations. For abbreviations see Table 5.7.

Latitude predicted the use of informal external support, though only at the second step after attention (Table 5.8). For IES, individual latitude scores emerged as a significant predictor (Table 5.14), thus providing an evidence for a differentiated unit. Besides this, the individual LT scores also predicted the use of personalized exchange and reasoning when put together with the group scores. Group scores did not predict the use of any influence strategies.

No doubt, the inflated results providing evidence for individual scores can be attributed, to some extent, to common method variance. All the same, a look at the four tables (Tables 5.11 through 5.14) shows that all the individual quality of exchange scores that predicted the use of influence strategies were highly significant. Thus, if there were minor differences in the results for individual and group scores, the assertion for any one level would have been shaky, but such vast differences in the two results indicate an individual level of analysis, despite common method variance.

One point needs to be mentioned here. The present results are only an evidence against averages and for individual levels of analysis. We are not asserting a within-group (i.e., group parts level) variation, as the individual scores are not represented in terms of groups (i.e., as deviations from group scores).

Comments

Broadly speaking, the use of both the upward and the downward influence strategies are predicted by the quality of exchange as a measure of leadership. Ansari (1990) conducted an exhaustive study of leadership styles in relation to upward and downward influence strategies. It needs to be noted here that though the leadership styles (of the leaders) and leadership behavior (as perceived by the subordinates) dimensions are taken from the average conceptualization, the relationship between the influence strategies and leadership orientations (behaviors or styles) is essentially at the individual level. The relationship is evaluated through stepwise regression where the individual responses on different dimensions are put in the regression equation. Thus, the results of this study too are an evidence for the individual level. Much in line with this, the results of the present study too find connection between leadership and influence strategies. In the present study, the measures developed on the basis of exchanges and interactions between a leader and a member significantly predict the use of influence strategies by the two (the leader and the member).

It is of interest to note that, in Study 1, PC was a better predictor for downward influence strategies; but for the upward strategies, affect emerged as a better predictor. In essence, the use of particular tactics by the leader is guided by on-the-job activities of the subordinates (contribution) but the use of strategies by the member is more a function of their (members') affective orientation towards the leader. Second, the interaction effects of PC and AF were significant neither for the upward nor for the downward influence strategies, in general. However, from both the perspectives, informal external support was predicted by the interaction of PC and AF, and from both the perspectives, low PC and low AF disclosed the maximum use of IES. But, so far as minimum use of IES is concerned, leaders' perspective (downward) was guided by PC and the members' perspective (upward) was guided by AF—a corroboration of the previous observation.

Finally, the individual scores of QEx were better predictors of influence strategies in general than the group scores, providing a rather strong evidence for the VDL.

In essence, hence, power and influence in the context of leadership is relevant both for the leaders (downward) and for the members (upward). Further, power and influence dynamics has variations within groups and the right entity to focus on is group-parts. Undoubtedly the hierarchy in organizations provides for a readymade exercise of power by the leader, but the members too exercise power over leaders, and there is evidence for a two-way influence process. Within a group (under a leader), the members have a different degree of power over (extent of influence), and also different bases of power for the leader which is a function of the quality of exchange between the two. Similarly, the leader too has a different degree of power over and also different bases of power for the member. Thus, in the context of leadership, power dynamics need to be studied at this level.

Other Outcome Variables

The Background

The role of leadership in subordinates' affective and behavioral experiences is well recognized. Almost all the theories and conceptualizations have studied this relationship. We shall briefly review how different theorizations have studied these outcome variables.

The earliest conceptualization of leadership in terms of authoritarian and democratic styles also correlated the two styles with different outcomes. Studies have been conducted to show the strength of each in predicting the performance of the subordinates.

Results provide evidence for both the dimensions. Some (e.g., Torrance, 1953) reported autocratic style to be more effective; others (e.g., Argyle, Gardner, & Ciofi, 1958) found democratic style to be more effective; still others (e.g., Ziller, 1957) reported that none of the two styles was significantly related to criterion measures.

Studies have also been conducted to see the effect of these two styles on satisfaction. Most studies (e.g., Ziller, 1957) report the superiority of the democratic style in predicting higher employee satisfaction. All the same, some studies (e.g., White, 1963) have discovered that there is no difference between autocratic and democratic styles, so far as subordinate satisfaction is concerned.

The effects of directive and participative leaderships on subordinate performance, commitment, and satisfaction have also been studied. Subordinate performance has been understood in terms of the quality of decisions and productivity. Group decisions are believed to be superior to the decisions made by an average member of that group. In line with this, the quality of decision under participative style has been reported to be better (Blake & Mouton, 1962) but the results for productivity are mixed, with some (e.g., Schumer, 1962) reporting the superiority of directive leadership and others (e.g., Lawrence & Smith, 1955) claiming the superiority of the participative style. An optimum level of participation seems to be effective in productivity; participation above or below that level affects performance adversely (Likert, 1959). So far as subordinate satisfaction is concerned, mostly participative style has been shown to be positively related to satisfaction (e.g., Preston & Heintz, 1949). However, some results are mixed with respect to subordinate satisfaction—for example, Farrow, Valenzi, and Bass (1980) found both the styles to be positively related to subordinate satisfaction. Employee commitment, loyalty, and job involvement too have been shown to be positively correlated with the participative style (e.g., Kahn & Tannenbaum, 1957).

Task and relationship orientations of the leader too have been studied in determining subordinate performance and satisfaction. Some studies (e.g., Pandey, 1976) have shown relationship-oriented leadership to be a superior predictor of follower performance, others (e.g., Litwin, 1968) found the task-oriented leader to be more effective. Besides the independent effects of the two, their joint effect has also been reported to significantly predict subordinate performance. High task and high relation orientations of a leader,

according to Blake and Mouton (1962), positively affect the performance—a finding corroborated by others as well (e.g., Kahn &
Katz, 1953). For subordinate satisfaction, generally, relationship-
oriented leadership has been found to be more effective (e.g. Mann
& Hoffman, 1960).

The two dimensions of leader behavior—consideration and initiating structure—developed in the Ohio State Studies too have been
shown to affect subordinates' outcomes. Both the dimensions have
been shown to be positively related to satisfaction (House & Filley,
1971), effectiveness (Fleishman & Simmons, 1970), and productivity (Lawshe & Nagle, 1953). Studies have also reported a curvili-
near relationship between the two dimensions and subordinate's
experiences. Fleishman and Harris (1962) observed the effect of
initiating structure and consideration on employee turnover and
greivances. They report that high and medium degrees of consideration coupled with low structure showed the lowest rates of employees' turnover and grievances.

The effect of different styles as a function of situational contingencies too has been explored. Patchen (1962), for example, showed
that directive supervision, in a cohesive group whose leader was
seen as a rewarding figure, had a high output. Centrality of problem (Bass & Ryterband, 1979), communication networks (Shaw,
1954), etc. too have been taken as situational contingencies, besides leader–member relations, position power (of the leader), and
task structure.

Thus, all the major theorizations understand and explain leadership in terms of subordinate outcomes.

Some Conjectures

In Chapter 1, we discussed the outcomes (consequences) studied
in the VDL framework. The review suggests that the previous researches have provided evidence for dyadic leadership and they
too have predicted the members' outcomes.

In view of the brief review of literature in the last section and
also in Chapter 1 (consequences of VDL), we take the following
outcome variables: satisfaction (Extrinsic [ES] and Intrinsic [IS];
commitment (CO); intent to leave (IL); and unit effectiveness (UE).
Intent to leave was taken in Study 1 only, and unit effectiveness in

Study 2 only. Extrinsic satisfaction, intrinsic satisfaction, and commitment were taken in both the studies.

The following three general hypotheses are proposed:

H5.6: Members' outcomes are a function of their quality of exchange.

H5.7: Members' outcomes are a function of the interaction of perceived contribution and affect.

H5.8: Members' outcomes are better predicted by their individual (VDL) as compared to the average (ALS) quality of exchange scores.

All the outcome variables are the subordinates' own perception, included in it is the unit effectiveness. It is hypothesized that the individual perception (of the subordinates) of unit effectiveness is a function of the individual quality of exchange. Hence, it is not a measure of the objective performance of the work-group.

Results and Discussion

Independent Effects of Quality of Exchange

The independent effects of QEx were measured both in Study 1 and Study 2.

Study 1 Results

Perceived contribution, affect, and leader–member exchanges (LMX) were the three measures of quality of exchange used as predictors in Study 1. The criterion measures (outcomes) in this study were—Extrinsic Satisfaction (ES), Intrinsic Satisfaction (IS), Commitment (CO), and Intent to Leave (IL). The zero-order correlations between predictors and criterion measures are reported in Table 5.5. The stepwise regression results for this study are reported in Table 5.15. Clearly, the two quality of interaction dimensions (perceived contribution and affect) did not predict any of the four outcome variables. However, LMX predicted intrinsic satisfaction and commitment (though not very strongly, $p < .05$). Both the outcomes are high, if LMX is high. Obviously, high leader–member exchanges predict greater intrinsic satisfaction and commitment of the subordinates. If LMX is high, the subordinate is naturally involved in collaboration on unstructured jobs and consequently the commitment too is high. As mentioned earlier (Chapter 4), leadership is a proximal representation of the organization for the subordinates. On the whole, the general commitment for the organization, hence, gets influenced by the nature of immediate leadership interactions.

We noted in Chapter 1 that the subordinates' intent to leave could not be predicted consistently by LMX theorization. This study too failed to find any significant results of this relationship. The employee withdrawal process (or intent) seems to be following some other rules. This does not mean that the nature of immediate leadership does not affect this outcome but independently, probably, it is not sufficient to explain enough variance.

Study 2 Results

In Study 2, intent to leave was dropped and the perception of unit effectiveness was added as a criterion variable. Besides the two dimensions of quality of interaction (PC and AF), attention (AT) and latitude (LT) were also taken as predictors (LMX was dropped). The results of zero-order correlation and stepwise regression are reported in Tables 5.7 and 5.16, respectively.

Extrinsic satisfaction in this study is predicted by perceived contribution, but attention also adds significantly to the variance. Perceived contribution and attention both are the measures of exchanges on actual job situations. Since extrinsic satisfaction concerns the satisfaction with external and actual job conditions, the results seem justified. Similarly, intrinsic satisfaction is predicted best by affect but perceived contribution adds significantly to it following the same line of argument; intrinsic satisfaction is the deeper satisfaction and is likely to have strong affective component. Thus, the prediction of intrinsic satisfaction by affect (mainly) is quite understandable. Perceived contribution too adds to this result positively, which means that for intrinsic satisfaction both the interaction on the jobs with the leader and affect for the leader together operate. Commitment is best predicted by attention. This looks like an exchange situation. The leader gives attention to the member and the member responds with greater commitment. The perception of unit effectiveness is predicted best by attention but

Table 5.15

Stepwise Regression Results—Members' Quality of Exchange
(Predictors) and Their Outcome Variables (Study 1)

Predictors				
	Criterion	PC	AF	LMX
ES				
	R	.34	.36	.37
	R^2 change	.12	.01	.00
	Beta	.17	.12	.13
	Order	1	2	3
IS				
	R	.39	.39	.38
	R^2 change	.00	.00	.14
	Beta	.12	.06	.25[b]
	Order	2	3	1
CO				
	R	.39	.40	.38
	R^2 change	.01	.00	.15
	Beta	.12	.08	.25[b]
	Order	2	3	1
IL				
	R	.18	.20	.20
	R^2 change	.03	.01	.00
	Beta	−.15	−.10	.02
	Order	1	2	3

Note: $N = 152$; b $p < .05$; PC = Perceived Contribution; AF = Affect; LMX = Leader–Member Exchanges; ES = Extrinsic Satisfaction; IS = Intrinsic Satisfaction; CO = Commitment; IL = Intent to Leave.

latitude also adds significantly to this prediction. Essentially, a unit is perceived to be more effective if the quality of exchange (measured in terms of attention and latitude) is better from the members' perspective.

In essence, thus, the outcomes of extrinsic satisfaction, intrinsic satisfaction, commitment, and unit effectiveness (perceived) are all a positive function of the quality of exchange between a leader and a member. Next, we see the interaction effect of PC and AF.

Interaction Effect of Perceived Contribution and Affect

The interaction effect of PC and AF on the outcome variables (like influence strategies) was tested in Study 1 only. Thus the interaction

Table 5.16
Stepwise Regression Results—Members' Quality of Exchange (Predictors) and Their Outcome Variables (Study 2)

Predictors	Criterion	PC	AF	AT	LT
ES					
	R	.61	*	.58	*
	R² change	.03	*	.34	*
	Beta	.28[b]	*	.35[a]	*
	Order	2	*	1	*
IS					
	R	.57	.53	*	*
	R² change	.04	.28	*	*
	Beta	.28[a]	.34[a]	*	*
	Order	2	1	*	*
CO					
	R	*	*	.66	*
	R² change	*	*	.43	*
	Beta	*	*	.66[a]	*
	Order	*	*	1	*
UE					
	R	*	*	.74	.76
	R² change	*	*	.54	.03
	Beta	*	*	.48[a]	.31[a]
	Order	*	*	1	2

Note: $N = 96$; a $p < .01$; b $p < .05$; PC = Perceived contribution; AF = Affect; AT = Attention; LT = Latitude; ES = Extrinsic Satisfaction; IS = Intrinsic Satisfaction; CO = Commitment; UE = Unit Effectiveness. * Tolerance level insufficient for further computations.

effects, through hierarchical regression were evaluated for ES, IS, CO, and IL.

The hierarchical regression results are reported in Table 5.17 and the corresponding means are reported in Table 5.18. The regression results reveal that the interaction is not significant for any outcome variables. The results are just like that of the influence strategies. The consistent failure of the interaction hypothesis to yield any outcome variables (leaders' influence strategies, members' influence strategies, and their other outcome variables) leads one to doubt the validity and strength of the interaction hypothesis. Finally, we move on to average *vs* individual test of quality of exchange.

Table 5.17

Hierarchical Regression Results—Members' Outcomes as a Function of the Interaction of Their Perceived Contribution and Affect (Study 1)

	PC[a]	(.25[a], .11)
ES	AF	(.15, .01)
	PC × AF	(−.03, .00)
	PC	(.23, .12)
IS	AF	(.13, .01)
	PC × AF	(−.11, .01)
	PC	(.23[a], .12)
CO	AF	(.14, .01)
	PC × AF	(−.10, .01)
	PC	(−.12[a], .03)
IL	AF	(−.10, .01)
	PC × AF	(.03, .00)

Note: $N = 152$; a $p < .01$; b $p < .05$; For abbreviations, see Table 5.15. Figures in parantheses are beta coefficients and R^2 change, respectively.

Table 5.18

Mean Scores—Members' Outcome Variables as a Function of the Interaction of Their Perceived Contribution and Affect (Study 1)

	PC AF	Low	High
ES	Low	16.01	17.38
	High	16.17	18.50
IS	Low	17.67	20.54
	High	18.61	21.00
CO	Low	43.45	50.38
	High	45.33	56.67
IL	Low	4.68	4.77
	High	4.89	3.00

Note: Same as Table 5.15.

Average vs Individual Quality of Exchange as Predictors

After evaluating the independent and interaction effects of quality of exchange measures, we now turn to the average *vs* non-average test. The procedure for these outcome variables is the same as for influence strategies.

For this purpose, data from Study 2 were taken, as it provided for reasonably big work-groups. The group and individual scores of the quality of exchange measures (PC, AF, AT, and LT) were put as predictors in a stepwise hierarchical regression. The regression results for PC, AF, AT, and LT are reported in Tables 5.19, 5.20, 5.21, and 5.22, respectively.

As is evident from the results, the individual scores (of all the four QEx measures) emerge as *much* stronger predictors of different outcomes. All the four outcome variables (ES, IS, CO, and UE) are best predicted by individual scores of all the four predictors (PC, AF, AT, and LT) (see Tables 5.19, 5.20, 5.21 and 5.22). However, the

Table 5.19

Stepwise Regression Results—Members' Perceived Contribution (Group and Individual Scores as Predictors) and Their Outcome Variables (Study 2)

Predictors	Criterion	PC(Id)	PC(Gr)
ES			
	R	.57	.59
	R^2 change	.33	.03
	Beta	.49[a]	.18[a]
	Order	1	2
IS			
	R	.50	*
	R^2 change	.25	*
	Beta	.50[a]	*
	Order	1	*
CO			
	R	.59	*
	R^2 change	.35	*
	Beta	.59[a]	*
	Order	1	*
UE			
	R	.59	.62
	R^2 change	.34	.03
	Beta	.68[a]	.18[b]
	Order	1	2

Note: $N = 96$; a $p < .01$; b $p < .05$; Gr = Group Scores; Id = Individual Scores. For other abbreviations see Table 5.16. * Tolerance level insufficient for further computations.

Table 5.20

Stepwise Regression Results—Members' Affect (Group and Individual Scores as Predictors) and Their Outcome Variables (Study 2)

Predictors	Criterion	AF(Id)	AF(Gr)
ES			
	R	.49	*
	R^2 change	.24	*
	Beta	.49[a]	*
	Order	1	*
IS			
	R	.52	*
	R^2 change	.27	*
	Beta	.52[a]	*
	Order	1	*
CO			
	R	.57	*
	R^2 change	.32	*
	Beta	.57[a]	*
	Order	1	*
UE			
	R	.62	*
	R^2 change	.38	*
	Beta	.62[a]	*
	Order	1	*

Note: $N = 96$; a $p < .01$; b $p < .05$; Gr = Group Scores; Id = Individual Scores. For other abbreviations see Table 5.16. * Tolerance level insufficient for further computations.

prediction of extrinsic satisfaction and unit effectiveness by perceived contribution creates an equivocal (reject) condition (see Table 5.19), as both the individual and the group scores significantly predict these two outcome variables.

Clearly, there is a strong evidence for individual-level predictions as against the group for all the quality of exchange measures. The subordinates' behavioral and affective outcomes are, hence, a function of their individual interaction with the leader.

Comments

As has been mentioned in Chapter 1, whereas relatively softer outcome variables (like satisfaction, commitment, etc.) have been

Table 5.21

Stepwise Regression Results—Members' Attention (Group and Individual Scores as Predictors) and Their Outcome Variables (Study 2)

Predictors	Criterion	AT(Id)	AT(Gr)
ES			
	R	.58	*
	R^2 change	.34	*
	Beta	.58[a]	*
	Order	1	*
IS			
	R	.47	*
	R^2 change	.22	*
	Beta	.47[a]	*
	Order	1	*
CO			
	R	.66	*
	R^2 change	.43	*
	Beta	.66[a]	*
	Order	1	*
UE			
	R	.74	*
	R^2 change	.54	*
	Beta	.74[a]	*
	Order	1	*

Note: $N = 96$; a $p < .01$; b $p < .05$; Gr = Group Scores; Id = Individual Scores. For other abbreviations see Table 5.16. * Tolerance level insufficient for further computations.

predicted by VDL conceptualization, harder measures like employee performance and turnover (intent to leave) have not been. In the present study, too, the only hard outcome variable (IL) could not be predicted by quality of exchange. However, the relative strength of average and VDL theorizations, for predicting intent to leave could not be tested as data in Study 1 were not sufficient to conduct this analysis. Vecchio et al.'s (1986) explanation for the failure of QEx to predict IL seems specious. They say, just as Mobley and his associates (Mobley, 1977; Mobley, Griffeth, Hand, & Meglino, 1979) have identified a series of intermediate processes (affective and cognitive) between employee perception and turnover, a similar (though unidentified) process might mediate quality of exchange and intent to leave (or turnover). We have already said that

Table 5.22

Stepwise Regression Results—Members' Latitude (Group and Individual Scores as Predictors) and Their Outcome Variables (Study 2)

Predictors	Criterion	LT(Id)	LT(Gr)
ES			
	R	.55	*
	R² change	.30	*
	Beta	.55ᵃ	*
	Order	1	*
IS			
	R	.42	*
	R² change	.18	*
	Beta	.42ᵃ	*
	Order	1	*
CO			
	R	.60	*
	R² change	.36	*
	Beta	.60ᵃ	*
	Order	1	*
UE			
	R	.71	*
	R² change	.50	*
	Beta	.71ᵃ	*
	Order	1	*

Note: $N = 96$; a $p < .01$; b $p < .05$; Gr = Group Scores; Id = Individual Scores. For other abbreviations see Table 5.16. * Tolerance level insufficient for further computations.

QEx when studied in conjunction with other processes might predict employee turnover or their intent to leave. Thus, the need is to identify these intermediate processes and the connections between them. The results, however, reveal that the other outcome variables for the members do get influenced by their quality of exchange.

The role and importance of unit differentiation in studying subordinates' behavior and feelings cannot be denied. The need now is to incorporate this fact with other important organizational processes to have a complete understanding of employees attitudes, feelings, and behaviors.

◄ Chapter 6 ►

Dyadic Interactions:
Making the Connection

This chapter is an attempt to provide an overall understanding of 'quality of interaction.' It specifically aims at integrating the various analyses performed in the last three chapters. Findings are discussed in the global perspective as well as in the Indian perspective. While doing so, managerial implications of the findings are discussed, potential limitations of the two surveys are presented, and recommendations for future research are highlighted.

The first part of the chapter deals with the integration of results. Findings are discussed in the first three sections. The preponderance of hierarchy in the Indian value system leads to unit differentiation. The nature of exchanges—the inputs and the outputs—in the Indian setting too are discussed. The next part deals with the implications of the present work. In the first section, the implications for the researchers are discussed. These implications draw heavily from the discussion in the last part. Essentially the focus is on exploring and understanding VDL in the Indian context. It is felt that though the process of unit differentiation is universal, the operating factors might be different for different cultures. In the next section of this part, the implications for leadership training are discussed. Essentially, the need to incorporate the fact of unit differentiation in different training techniques is emphasized.

Finally, in the last part of the chapter, some potential limitations of the present studies are presented.

Integration of the Findings

In Chapter 1, it was mentioned that there were three broad aims of the present work: *(i)* to develop a comprehensive measure of the interactions between a leader and a member, *(ii)* to identify relevant antecedent factors that determine the quality of this interaction, and *(iii)* to see the impact (consequences) of the quality of interaction on the work dynamics (influence tactics) of both leaders and members, and the job related behaviors and attitudes of the subordinates. The findings of these three objectives are reported in Chapters 3, 4, and 5, respectively. We will take up the findings related to the three aims separately and try to discuss them in the Indian context.

Nature of Quality of Interaction

Throughout the manuscript, we have been contending for a dyadic approach to study leadership. In Chapter 3, a two-dimensional measure of quality of interaction was developed. We have discussed the two dimensions—perceived contribution and affect—in that chapter. It was also noted that the work-unit under a leader gets differentiated, wherein the differences are reported both by the leader and the members. In the Indian context, it is worthwhile to note that broadly the Indian (equated with Hindu) social system has the concept of hierarchy inherent in it (Roland, 1980) and, in general, the social system (culture) is structured in terms of superior–subordinate relationships, so much so, that even peers and friends are ranked in a hierarchical order (J.B.P. Sinha, 1990). This means that Indians, by and large, have a tendency to grade, divide, and subdivide. The rule of hierarchy follows everywhere even in a work-unit under a leader. In Chapter 1, we pointed out that unit differentiation under a leader is imperative given the transience of the environment. This point is not refuted at all from the global organizational perspective. What we are trying here is to understand and explain the results from the organizational members' perspective. Our analysis would mean that even if the environment was static, the Indian manager will differentiate between subordinates, given the social values. The effect of transient environment gets compounded when such values are dominant. Later we will see how these prevalent values also act as the determinants of unit differentiation (hierarchy). Further, it is interesting to note that the differentiation (hierarchy) is maintained through 'affective reciprocity' (Roland, 1984). The reciprocal nature of *affect* in a leader–member dyad, too, was established in Chapter 4. We do not mean to say that a leader–member dyad is a microcosm of broad and global social phenomena, but the influence of the latter on the former cannot be denied. Kumar and Singh (1976) have given two dimensions—personal–impersonal, own–others—to understand the construct system of an Indian manager. Interestingly, affective reciprocity exists for people who are in the own and personal quadrant. The relationship with these IN-Group members is characterized with reciprocal affection (J.B.P. Sinha, 1990). On the other hand, relationship with impersonal-others is devoid of this affect. In Chapters 1 and 3, it was mentioned that perceived contribution and affect both are high for higher quality dyads where the collaboration is more.

Hence, the emergence of perceived contribution and affect in the Indian context is in line with the above mentioned arguments. Thus, we see that the Indian milieu provides us with a readymade pattern of differentiation with perceived contribution and affect as the key determinants of this differentiation.

Though the theme of hierarchy in the Indian value system is much recognized, it is surprising to note that the concept of hierarchy within a work-group has not been given enough attention.

It was mentioned in Chapter 1 that unit differentiation occurs because of differential exchanges between a leader and different members. In the Indian context, J.B.P. Sinha (1990, p. 39) notes that in the IN-Groups (high quality dyads), 'the superiors are expected to have warmth, affection, care, nurturance, etc. for the subordinates or juniors who must reciprocate by being loyal, trustworthy, respectful, dependent, etc.' The exchanges are clear. But these are the exchanges that typify the cultural mien. In actual work settings, this exchange of affection and deference takes place through real job problems and through role episodes (see Chapter 1, Figure 1.1). So, this is the nature of unit differentiation in Indian organizations. Next, we shift our attention to the antecedents of this differentiation.

Antecedents of Quality of Interaction

In the last section, we noticed that it is not only the environmental contingencies that force a unit differentiation, but also the cultural values that work towards this differentiation. In Chapter 4, we identified some antecedents of quality of interaction (exchange). Essentially, we talked of three interactions—personal orientations with personal orientations, leadership orientations with leadership orientations, personal orientations with perceived climate. It was noted that whereas the first interaction did not yield significant results, the last two did. Although the two interactions did yield significant results and we have discussed those results in Chapter 5, the antecedents have to be identified at a deeper grassroot level. Indian reality needs to be identified at this stage. No doubt, the person–environment interactions are important, an understanding of the Indian psyche and Indian values should be a more fruitful attempt. In the present work, we have established that the personal orientations of the two parties (in general) are not really very important and they should be left alone. The personal orientation of the leader is important only so far as it sets a particular environment for the subordinates to work in. The subordinates choose themselves in or out of such situations depending upon their own personal orientations.

We failed to identify any antecedent conditions that might determine the quality of interaction from the leaders' perspective. According to our model in Chapter 1, ideally a leader should choose a competent (efficient and effective) subordinate to collaborate on unstructured tasks. The leaders will do so if their prime concern is to get the job done. The selection of people, in such cases, into IN- and OUT-Groups will follow a rational process wherein the competence of the subordinates is a valued resource. We noted, however, that the Indian social values too work towards differentiation and when the aim of the leader is to differentiate for personal benefits (not organizational), obviously the criteria for choosing subordinates (into IN- and OUT-Groups) will be different. As J.B.P. Sinha (1990, p. 36) notes, in general, 'family, relatives, friends, coworkers, caste men, persons speaking the same language, belonging to same area or religion or the country may be the ingroups.'

Clearly, selection of subordinates in the IN-Group on these criteria, overlooks the organizational goals totally. Thus, though the fact of unit differentiation is accepted, it is the antecedent conditions that will predict the relative effectiveness or ineffectiveness of this differentiation.

In Chapter 1, an ideal situation and antecedents of unit differentiation was identified. As mentioned earlier, these antecedent conditions become pathological if the concerns of both the leaders and the members are not organizational. But irrespective of the antecedents, the process of selecting subordinates into IN- and OUT-Groups is the same (through role development). In a pathological case, the members are chosen (into IN/OUT-Group) on essentially demographic characteristics (like caste, religion, region, etc.) straightaway, and these people have a major share in strategic decision-making and other vital organizational processes. Obviously, this will have direct implications for organizational effectiveness. The need, hence, is to identify these variables and relate them to the effectiveness of organization, in general, and the leaders, in particular.

Consequences of Quality of Interaction

In Chapter 5, the consequences of the quality of interaction were discussed. The results were discussed under two heads—social influence processes and other outcome variables.

Leadership has been conceptualized as a reciprocal influence process. In this light, the identification of actual influence processes becomes a must. In line with our conceptualization of unit differentiation, the influence processes need to be studied at the dyadic level in terms of leaders' interaction with individual subordinates. The use of influence tactics, both from the leader and the member perspectives, shows variation within a work-group.

The use of personalized exchange by both (leader and member) to influence each other has special relevance in the Indian context. Preference for personalized relationship is a dominant value for Indians. Hence, the use of personal relationships is a valued outcome. The use of this tactic, hence, for the IN-Group members by the leader and vice versa stands validated. The use of other tactics in the IN- and OUT-Groups has already been discussed. Thus, leadership and power dynamics need to be studied at the work-group level with a focus on within-group variations. The power play within and between work-groups will help in understanding organizational dynamics.

Further, the attitudes, feelings, and behaviors of the members in an organization are closely linked with their leader, specifically, with their individual interaction with the leader. As J.B.P. Sinha (1990) notes, the group norms and values for the IN-Group members are often different for and sometimes opposite to that of the OUT-Group members. Clearly, a perception of this difference by the members leads to differing experiences. Since motivation, satisfaction, commitment, etc. of the employees are a reflection of the overall organizational effectiveness, it is a must that strong predictive correlates of these variables be identified and explicated. Mostly, leadership research (in the average framework) has shown mixed and inconclusive results. Although the research concerning the VDL approach is limited, unit-differentiation seems to be a more practical and realistic understanding.

The need, hence, is to study dyadic exchanges in the Indian setting. In the next section, we briefly present an integrated framework based on the last three sections. This may be taken up in the future research.

VDL in the Indian Setting

In Indian organizations, we see that it is not only the demands placed on the organizations (as stated in Chapter 1) that lead to the differentiation of work-unit under a leader, but also the social values of the people in organizations work towards this differentiation. Undoubtedly, the industrial activity in India has been rapidly expanding with the importation of western technology and know-how. This places extra developmental demands on the organization (in line with our argument in Chapter 1), which makes unit differentiation a must. These organizations are made up of people who also believe in hierarchical differentiation (of the work units). But the aims of the two are *usually* not the same. We have large technical organizations modeled after western lines but the people have Indian values. Thus, the need is to identify the points of similarity and differences between the two. An exhaustive search of these variables will throw light on the actual functioning of these organizations.

Further, we mentioned that there are unique exchanges between the leader and different members. The nature of exchanges in the Indian setting is of immense importance in understanding the quality of interaction in leader–member dyads. J.B.P. Sinha (1990) identifies the nature of exchanges in terms of *sneh–shradha* (Affection–Deference). It is interesting to note that though the so-called IN-Group members enjoy a special elevated status, the *status quo* may be maintained even in high quality dyads. Despite the fact that leaders and members are interdependent for getting the work done, the exchange terms for the two are supposed to be different. Whereas the leader gives warmth, support, care, and nurturance, the subordinates may respond by being respectful, loyal, and dependent. Future studies can focus on these dimensions of exchanges to better understand the nature of dyadic interactions.

Implications

Issues for the Researchers

In the last part, we tried to evaluate VDL in the Indian context. The discussion leads to an identification of different antecedent or contingency factors and exchange processes. Further, researchers can attempt to combine the average theorizations with dyadic ones. The general orientations of the leaders (work or relationship) reflect their style of working. These styles can define the leaders' preferred antecedent conditions. Thus, whereas a work-oriented leader might look for job-related competence in subordinates, a relationship-oriented leader will look for interpersonal qualities. Essentially, if leadership research is to yield some relevant insights, the level of analysis has to be given due importance.

Further, the VDL model needs to be expanded. As was mentioned in Chapter 1, VDL has been extended in some contexts. Although the extensions seem to be theoretically sound, there is little empirical attempt to validate the extension. Such an extension might provide us with linkages in understanding the other 'hard' outcomes of the employees (e.g., intent to leave).

Once the fact of unit differentiation is acknowledged, it has some special significance for practitioners and managers.

Implications for the Managers and Practitioners

It has been recognized that educating people in the right way helps in the development of leadership skills. This fact has implications for leadership training. The relevance, effectiveness, and importance of leadership training is well established. We will take up different training techniques and see how VDL can be incorporated in them. But before that it has to be deciphered whether unit differentiation is desirable in the interest of all the parties (the organization and its members). Since leader–member interactions are related to employee satisfaction, commitment, and other behaviors, it is desirable that these dyadic interactions be such that they improve satisfaction, etc. of the subordinates. In brief, programs designed to improve these dyadic interactions will lead to better outcomes for members with low quality of interaction. This concept can be incorporated in different training procedures, both on- and off-the-jobs.

To begin with, the managers (as leaders) have to be made aware of this fact of unit differentiation through lectures and discussions. Providing the relevant information will stimulate relevant thinking in managers.

Role playing is yet another technique of training in which the fact of unit differentiation can be incorporated. Through this process leaders and managers can be made aware of this fact (role playing as diagnostic process). Group discussion following the role playing might help in a proper diagnosis of exchanges. Not only the role players but the other trainee observers might also gain from this insight. The concept of dyadic exchanges can be introduced through the simulation techniques of in-basket training and games. Sensitivity training should be an important tool especially in the Indian setting, because affect dimension is likely to be very strong. Sensitivity training can be aimed at greater sensitivity towards subordinates with low LMX. The trainees' (leaders') attitudes, perceptions, and behavior can be changed in consonance with our theory of dyadic exchanges. Similarly, this concept can be incorporated in behavior modeling techniques, as well.

There has been very little use of this theory in leadership training. This is probably because the theory is relatively recent and has seen little empirical work. The effectiveness of leadership intervention based on the LMX or VDL model is reported by Scandura and Graen (1984). They reported that such an intervention improved the job satisfaction and leadership satisfaction of the subordinates who had low LMX before intervention. The need, therefore, is to recognise this vital aspect of leadership and incorporate it in training programs for better results.

A Word of Caution

The present work is not devoid of limitations. The first emanates from the nature of the work. We are working with a developmental concept (quality of exchange) and the best way to study it is through a longitudinal study. This work takes the freeze snap-shot view at the time of the researcher's entry into the organization. However, the stability of these exchanges over time has been reported (e.g., Wakabayashi & Graen, 1984; Wakabayashi et al., 1988). Thus, the results of cross-sectional studies of this kind can also provide useful insights.

The second limitation is concerned with the two samples employed in the two studies. The sample in Study 1 was a much larger sample ($N = 219$) as compared to the sample in Study 2 ($N = 122$). Thus, all those hypotheses that were tested in Study 2 only (though few) can be validated through larger and heterogeneous samples. However, the sample size in Study 2 too is not so small as the focus is on dyadic interactions, and the preferred analysis is based on a continuous scale where each and every score is of importance.

The third limitation deals with the nature of outcome variables taken in the present work. The hard outcome variables like performance, productivity, turnover, etc. were not incorporated in the study. Intent to leave came closest to this objective.

Fourth, we have conducted no analysis to study the proposed relationships in terms of the nature of the organizations studied. Future studies can explore the nature of dyadic exchange in different organizations in terms of ownership (public or private) and financial status (running in profit or losses), etc. It should be noted, however, that we employed four diverse organizations in Study 1 and just one large manufacturing organization in Study 2. The comparable results were found to be almost identical in both the studies.

Finally, one limitation of the study is its lack of major focus on Indian reality. The impact of Indian values and work culture on unit differentiation has not been explored in the present work. This is because these values and orientations need to be operationalized in work settings for them to be incorporated in any study of organizational behavior. Incorporating culture-specific issues in understanding dyadic quality of interaction may yield more realistic understanding of dyadic exchanges in a particular environment.

◄ Appendix I ►

Questionnaire for Study 1

Section I—Relationship

1. (PAL) In organizations individuals work with different people. Working with others is a must to achieve the organizational goal(s). In this process, the individual may interact differently with different people and with *one at a time*. We want you to evaluate your interaction with _____ in terms of the following questions. Please read each of the questions carefully and judge the *degree* to which it is true to the interaction between the *two* of you. Select the number of your choice (given below) and put it to the left of the statement in the space provided.

Very much	7
A good deal	6
Quite a bit	5
Somewhat	4
A little	3
Very little	2
Not at all	1

— (01L) How much is his/her work activity valuable to other members of your group?

— (02P) How much time does he/she spend on the jobs that are to be done together by you and him/her?

— (03A) How much affection do you have for each other?

— (04P) How much responsibility does he/she take for the jobs that are to be done jointly by you and him/her?

— (05L) How much help does he/she readily get from other group members in accomplishing the group tasks?

— (06P) How much is his/her contribution in terms of the viable solutions to the problems that are to be solved together by you and him/her?

— (07A) How much do you interact with each other off the job?

— (08L) How much is his/her work activity resisted by others?

— (09P) How much is his/her contribution to the quality of solutions on the jobs that are to be done together by you and him/her?

— (10A) How much liking do you have for each other?

— (11A) How much effort does he/she put in the jobs that are to be done together by you and him/her?

— (12L) How efficient is he/she considered on his/her job by other members of your group?

— (13A) How much do you help each other in personal matters?

— (14L) How much is he/she liked by other members of your group?

— (15P) How much is his/her contribution to the quantity of solutions on the jobs that are to be done together by you and him/her?

— (16A) How much advice do you seek from each other on personal problems?

— (17P) How efficient is his/her contribution on the jobs for which the two of you work together?

— (18L) How much is his/her work activity supported by other members of your group?

— (19A) How much do you discuss your personal matters with each other?

— (20L) How much is his/her work activity valued by other members of your group?

— (21P) How useful is his/her effort on the jobs that are to be done together by you and him/her?

— (22A) How much interest do you take in solving each other's problems?

— (23A) How much importance do you attach to each other's advice on personal matters?

— (24P) How much initiative does he/she take in solving the problems to be done together by you and him/her?

2. **(INF)** Below are described various ways of obtaining information about how you go about changing the mind (or opinion) of _____ so that he/she agrees with you. Please describe each statement, on a seven-point scale (given below) as to how *frequently* you use each of the following

items to influence him/her at work. Describe the statements in terms of what you do, not what you would like to do.

Never	1
Almost never	2
Seldom	3
Sometimes	4
Usually	5
Almost always	6
Always	7

— (01C) Call a staff meeting to back your request.
— (02A) Repeatedly remind him/her about what you want.
— (02I) Praise him/her with superlatives.
— (04W) Keep a straight face, conceal your emotions.
— (05S) Tell him/her that you have a lot of experience with such matters.
— (06S) Straightaway ask him/her to do what you want.
— (07M) Get your way by making him/her feel that it was his/her idea.
— (08P) Repeatedly ask him/her until he/she gives in.
— (09S) Show your knowledge of technical issues.
— (10R) Convince him/her by telling him/her the urgency and utility of the issue at hand.
— (11E) Offer an exchange of favor.
— (12W) Clamp up (become silent).
— (13P) Do personal favors for him/her.
— (14U) Appeal formally to higher ups to back your request.
— (15M) Distort or lie about reasons why he/she should do what you want.
— (16I) Ask him/her to do some task in a polite way.
— (17M) At times withhold some crucial information from him/her.
— (18C) Find others elsewhere in the organization who support your activities.
— (19I) Make him/her feel important.
— (20U) Obtain informal support of higher ups.
— (21R) Sometimes tell him/her the reasons for making the request.
— (22P) Help him/her even in personal matters.
— (23W) Back down quickly.
— (24E) Remind him/her of past favors you did for him/her.
— (25A) Set a time deadline to do what you ask.
— (26C) Bring some friends along to back your request.
— (27I) Even when you know you would not use his/her advice, you consult him/her.

— (28P) Repeatedly persuade him/her to comply with your arguments as they are the need of the time.

— (29M) Keep a record of his/her omissions and commissions.

— (30U) Get the support of some higher up to back your request.

— (31R) Tell him/her exactly why you need his/her help.

— (32I) Use the words that make him/her feel good.

— (33P) At times try to persuade him/her that your way is the best.

— (34M) Present your ideas in a disguised way.

— (35C) Get everyone else to agree with you before you make the request.

— (36E) Remind him/her how hard you had worked and it would only be fair for him/her to help you now.

— (37P) Help him/her by going out of your way when he/she is in need of help.

— (38R) Tell him/her the reasons why your plan is the best.

— (39U) Refer the matter to the higher authority if the situation so demands.

— (40S) Influence him/her with your competence.

— (41R) Argue your points logically.

— (42S) At times show your knowledge of the specific issue.

— (43W) Do nothing.

— (44E) Offer some personal sacrifice in exchange (e.g., doing part of his/her or others' job, etc.).

— (45A) Tell him/her exactly what is it that you want.

— (46P) Get your way by convincing him/her that your way is the best way.

— (47P) Go on asking persistently till he/she does what you want.

3. (LMX) The following questions relate to your immediate supervisor. Please answer them by ticking one of the four alternatives given with each question. Tick the alternative that describes best your relationship with your immediate supervisor.

(1) How flexible do *you* believe *your* supervisor is about evolving change in *your* job?
— (4) Supervisor is enthused about change.
— (3) Supervisor is lukewarm to change.
— (2) Supervisor sees little need to change.
— (1) Supervisor sees no need to change.

(2) Regardless of how much formal organizational authority *your* supervisor has built into his/her position, what are the chances that he/she would be personally inclined to use his/her power to help *you* solve problems in your work?

— (4) He certainly would.
— (3) Probably would.
— (2) Might or might not.
— (1) No.

(3) To what extent can *you* count on *your* supervisor to 'bail you out,' at his/her expense, when *you* really need him/her?
— (4) Certainly would.
— (3) Probably.
— (2) Might or might not.
— (1) No.

(4) How often do *you* take suggestions regarding your work to your supervisor?
— (4) Almost always.
— (3) Usually.
— (2) Seldom.
— (1) Never.

(5) How would you characterize *your* working relationship with your supervisor?
— (4) Extremely effective.
— (3) Better than average.
— (2) About average.
— (1) Less than average.

Section II—PAIR

Below are listed 20 statements that describe various things people do or try to do on their jobs. Please rate on a seven-point scale given below, how frequently each of the statements fits your action, and write the number of your choice on the small line to the left of the statement. Remember, there are no right or wrong answers. Please answer all questions frankly.

Never	1
Almost never	2
Seldom	3
Sometimes	4
Usually	5
Almost always	6
Always	7

— (01I) I consider myself a 'team player' at work.
— (02I) I go my own way at work, regardless of the opinion of others.

— (03P) I strive to be 'in command' when I am working in a group.
— (04R) I express my disagreements with others openly.
— (05I) In my work assignments, I try to be my own boss.
— (06P) I see an active role in the leadership of a group.
— (07I) I disregard rules and regulations that hamper my personal freedom.
— (08I) I try my best to work alone on a job.
— (09R) I find myself talking to those around me about non-business-related matters.
— (10A) I try very hard to improve on my past performance at work.
— (11A) I try to avoid any added responsibilities on my job.
— (12R) I prefer to do my own work and let others do theirs.
— (13R) I pay a good deal of attention to the feelings of others at work.
— (14A) I do my best work when job assignments are fairly difficult.
— (15P) I avoid trying to influence those around me to see things my way.
— (16A) I try to perform better than my co-workers.
— (17P) I strive to gain more control over the events around me at work.
— (18A) I take moderate risks and stick my neck out to get ahead at work.
— (19P) I find myself organizing and directing the activities of others.
— (20R) When I have a choice, I try to work in a group instead of by myself.

Section III—CL

The following set of statements is concerned with your perceptions and observations about the organization in which you are presently working. Please read each of them carefully and judge the extent to which you consider them to be true to your organization, and write the number of your choice in the space provided to the left of the statement.

Almost no extent	1
To a very small extent	2
To a small extent	3
To some extent	4
To a considerable extent	5
To a great extent	6
To a very great extent	7

— (01R) This organization encourages its employees to discuss non-business-related personal problems.

— (02A) In this organization, there is a feeling of pressure to continually improve individual and group performance.

— (03I) In this organization, control is assigned so that I have authority within my work area.

— (04P) This organization strives to be 'in command' while interacting with other organizations.

— (05R) This organization prefers group to individual projects and provides opportunities for its employees to interact among themselves.

— (06R) This organization pays a good deal of attention to the feelings of its employees.

— (07A) This organization stimulates and approves innovation and experimentation.

— (08A) In this organization we set fairly high standards for performance.

— (09P) This organization prefers to be its own boss, even where it needs assistance, or where a joint effort is required.

— (10I) In this organization, it is up to us to decide how our job should best be done.

— (11I) This organization wants us to be 'team players' rather than 'independent workers.'

— (12P) Status symbols are especially important for this organization and it uses them to gain influence over others.

— (13R) In this organization, the interpersonal communications among executives and managers are free and open.

— (14A) This organization discourages taking up of increased responsibilities by its members.

— (15A) In this organization, we are free to set our own performance goal.

— (16I) In this organization, there are opportunities for independent thoughts and actions on our jobs.

— (17P) This organization directs and organizes the activities of its members.

— (18I) In this organization, we have a great deal of freedom to decide how we do our job.

— (19R) There is a high degree of interpersonal trust among managers and executives in this organization.

— (20P) This organization provides a lot of power and control to upper-level management.

Section IV—Output

1. (SAT). Please indicate how satisfied you are on a seven-point scale with each of the following aspects of your job. Read each item carefully and put the number of your choice in the space provided to the left of the item.

Very dissatisfied	1
Dissatisfied	2
Slightly dissatisfied	3
Neutral	4
Slightly satisfied	5
Satisfied	6
Very satisfied	7

HOW SATISFIED ARE YOU WITH...

— (01) The fringe benefits you receive.
— (02) The friendliness of the people you work with.
— (03) The amount of freedom you have on your job.
— (04) The chances you have to learn new things.
— (05) The respect you receive from the people you work with.
— (06) The amount of pay you get.
— (07) The chances you have to do something that makes you feel good about yourself as a person.
— (08) The way you are treated by the people you work with.
— (09) The chances (times) you have to take part in making decisions.
— (10) The amount of job security you have.
— (11) The amount of personal growth and development you get in doing your job.
— (12) The feeling of worthwhile accomplishment you get in doing your job.
— (13) How secure things look for you in the future in this organization.
— (14) The amount of challenge in your job.
— (15) The chances to get to know other people while on the job.
— (16) The chances for advancement on your job.

2. (COM). Listed below are a series of statements that represent possible feelings that individuals might have for organizations for which they work. With respect to your own feeling about the particular organization for which you are now working, please indicate the degree of your agreement or disagreement with each statement.

Write the number of your choice in the blank beside each statement, based on the following scale.

Strongly disagree	1
Moderately disagree	2
Slightly disagree	3
Neither agree nor disagree	4
Slightly agree	5
Moderately agree	6
Strongly agree	7

— (1) I am willing to put in a great deal of effort beyond that normally expected in order to help this organization be successful.

— (2) I talk about this organization to my friends as a great organization to work for.

— (3) I would accept almost any type of job assignment in order to keep working for this organization.

— (4) I find that my values and the organization's values are very similar.

— (5) I am proud to tell others that I am a part of this organization.

— (6) I could just as well as be working for a different organization as long as the type of work were similar.

— (7) This organization really inspires the very best in me in the way of job performance.

— (8) Often, I find it difficult to agree with this organization's policies on important matters relating to its employees.

— (9) I really care about the fate of this organization.

Section V—Personal Data

(01) Your age _____ years.

(02) Educational Qualifications (Degree, Diploma, etc.) _____ .

(03) Your job title or designation _____ .

(04) For how many years have you been with your present organization? _____ .

(05) For how many years have you been working in your present position? _____ .

(06) How many promotions have you received in your professional career? _____ .

(07) Which of the following statements most clearly reflects your feelings about your future with this employer/organization?
   1. Definitely will not leave.
   2. Probably will not leave.

    3. Uncertain.
    4. Probably will leave.
    5. Definitely will leave.
(08) Do you expect to leave your job in the near future?
    1. Will definitely leave in the near future.
    2. The chances are quite good that I will leave.
    3. The situation is uncertain.
    4. The chances are very slight that I will leave.
    5. Definitely will not leave in the near future.

Once again thank you for your help!

◀ Appendix II ▶

Questionnaire for Study 2

Section I—PAI

Below are listed 15 statements that describe various things people do or try to do on their jobs. Please rate on a seven-point scale given below, how *frequently* each of the statements *fits* your action, and write the number of your choice on the small line to the left of the statement. Remember: There are no right or wrong answers. Please answer all questions frankly.

Never	1
Almost never	2
Seldom	3
Sometimes	4
Usually	5
Almost always	6
Always	7

— (01I)   I go my own way at work, regardless of the opinion of others.
— (02P)   I strive to be 'in command' when I am working in a group.
— (03I)   In my work assignments, I try to be my own boss.
— (04P)   I seek an active role in the leadership of a group.
— (05I)   I disregard rules and regulations that hamper my personal freedom.
— (06I)   I try my best to work alone on a job.
— (07A)   I try very hard to improve on my past performance at work.

— (08A) I try to avoid any added responsibilities on my job.
— (09A) I do my best work when job assignments are fairly difficult.
— (10A) I try to perform better than my co-workers.
— (11Ā) I strive to gain more control over the events around me at work.

Section II—CL

The following set of statements is concerned with your perceptions and observations about the organization in which you are presently working. Please read each of them carefully and judge the *extent* to which you consider it to be true to your organization, and write the number of your choice in the space provided to the left of the statement.

Almost no extent	1
To a very small extent	2
To a small extent	3
To some extent	4
To a considerable extent	5
To a great extent	6
To a very great extent	7

— (01A) In this organization, there is a feeling of pressure to continually improve individual and group performance.
— (02A) This organization stimulates and approves of innovation and experimentation.
— (03A) In this organization, we set fairly high standards for performance.
— (04P) This organization prefers to be its own boss, even where it needs assistance, or where a joint effort is required.
— (05I) In this organization, it is up to us to decide how our job should best be done.
— (06P) Status symbols are especially important for this organization and it uses them to gain influence over others.
— (07I) In this organization, we are free to set our own performance goals.
— (08I) In this organization, there are opportunities for independent thoughts and actions on our jobs.
— (09I) In this organization, we have a great deal of freedom to decide how we do our job.
— (10P) This organization provides a lot of power and control to upper-level management.

Section III—Personal Data

(01) Your age (please write in) _____ years.
(02) Educational Qualifications (Degree, Diploma, etc.) _____ .
(03) Your job title or designation _____ .
(04) For how many years have you been with your present organization? _____
(05) For how many years have you been working in your present position? _____ .
(06) How many promotions have you received in your professional career? _____ .

Section IV—Style

1. (LS). This scale is meant to find out the different ways a manager acts, feels, or prefers. Thus the following statements are about your behavior. Please read each of them carefully and decide how *frequently* it is true for you. Select the number of your choice, as given below, and put it on the small line to the left of the statement.

Never	1
Almost never	2
Seldom	3
Sometimes	4
Usually	5
Almost always	6
Always	7

— (01P) I often consult my subordinates.
— (02N) I take personal interest in the promotion of those subordinates who work hard.
— (03F) I keep important information to myself.
— (04P) I let my subordinates solve a problem jointly.
— (05N) I encourage my subordinates to assume greater responsibility on the job as they become more experienced.
— (06P) I treat my subordinates as equal.
— (07P) I go by the joint decisions of my group.
— (08F) I think that not all employees are capable of being officers.
— (09F) I am quite confident of being right in making decisions.
— (10N) I openly favor those who work hard.
— (11F) I keep an eye on what my subordinates do.

— (12N) I go out of my way to help those subordinates who maintain high standards of performance.
— (13P) I make my subordinates feel free even to disagree with me.
— (14N) I feel good when I find my subordinates eager to learn.
— (15F) I command my subordinates to do what I want.

Section V—(PS)

Listed below are three descriptions concerning the behavior of a manager.

Description A: He/she emphasizes obedience and respect for authority; makes decisions single-handedly; is very confident of his/her decisions being right; and keeps a close eye on his/her subordinates.

Description B: He/she is a task-and-efficiency-oriented manager; is a realist and wants to get the job done anyhow; and likes and encourages those subordinates who work hard.

Description C: He/she is people-oriented and encourages team work. Though he/she is quite concerned with efficiency, he/she cares more for the subordinates and helps them develop their individual worth.

Compare each pair of descriptions according to your preference. Allocate three points between the two alternative descriptions in each pair. Base your point allocation on your judgement of each description's relative preference to you. Thus, allocate the point between the first description and the second description (in each pair) based on the degree of your preference in the following fashion. Thus if you prefer A much more than B, then allocate 3 to A and 0 to B (as shown in box D). Similarly, if you prefer A slightly more than B, then assign 2 to A and 1 to B (see box C). And so on.

A	0		A	1		A	2		A	3
B	3		B	2		B	1		B	0
(a)			(b)			(c)			(d)	

Be sure that the numbers assigned to each pair add up to 3.

1) Compare A and B descriptions

A	—
B	—

2) Compare A and C descriptions

A	—
C	—

3) Compare B and C descriptions

C	—
B	—

Section VI—IR

1 (AT). The following questions relate to your interaction with your immediate superior. Please read each of them carefully and judge the degree to which it is present in your relationship with him/her, according to the scale given below. Write the number of your choice in the space provided to the left of the statement.

Almost none	1
A little	2
A fair amount	3
Quite a bit	4
A great deal	5

(1) How much information does he/she give to you about his/her assessment of your job performance?

(2) How much attention does he/she give to your feelings and needs?

(3) How much information does he/she give to you about the current and future state of your unit/division and your position in the unit?

(4) How much support does he/she give to your action and ideas?

(5) How much serious consideration does he/she give to your suggestions and ideas?

(2) (LT). Now rate the next five questions according to the following scale:

No chance	1
Probably no	2
Probably	3
Certainly	4

(1) In general, would he/she let you implement the changes that you wanted to make in your job?

(2) Would he/she tend to let you implement changes in your job if you had previously spoken to him/her about those changes?

(3) Would he/she tend to let you implement changes in your job even if you had not previously spoken to him/her about those changes?

(4) Would he/she tend to let you implement changes in your job as long as they had little impact on how he/she did his/her own job?

(5) Would he/she tend to let you implement changes in your job even if those changes had a major impact on how he/she did his/her own job?

Section VII—Relationship

1. (PA) In organizations individuals work with different people. Working with others is a must to achieve the organizational goal(s). In this process, the individual may interact differently with different people and with one at a time. We want you to evaluate your interaction with your immediate superior in terms of the following questions. Please read each of the questions carefully and judge the degree to which it is true to the interaction between the two of you. Select the number of your choice (given below) and put it to the left of the statement in the space provided.

Very much	7
A good deal	6
Quite a bit	5
Somewhat	4
A little	3
Very little	2
Not at all	1

(01P)   How much responsibility does he/she take for the jobs that are to be done jointly by you and him/her?

(02A)   How much do you interact with each other off the job?

(03A)   How much do you help each other in personal matters?

(04P)   How much is his/her contribution to the quantity of solutions on the jobs that are to be done together by you and him/her?

(05A)   How much advice do you seek from each other on personal problems?

(06P)   How efficient is his/her contribution on the jobs for which the two of you work together?

(07A)   How much do you discuss your personal matters with each other?

(08P)   How useful is his/her effort on the jobs that are to be done together by you and him/her?

(09A)   How much importance do you attach to each other's advice on personal matters?

(10P)   How much initiative does he/she take in solving the problems to be done together by you and him/her?

2. (INF) Below are described various ways of obtaining information about how you go about changing the mind (or opinion) of your immediate superior so that he/she agrees with you. Please describe each statement, on a seven-point scale (given below), as to how frequently you use it to influence him/her at work. Describe the statements in terms of what you do, not what you would like to do.

Never	1
Almost never	2
Seldom	3
Sometimes	4
Usually	5
Almost always	6
Always	7

(01C) Call a staff meeting to back your request.

(02I) Praise him/her with superlatives.

(03I) Get your way by making him/her feel that it was his/her idea.

(04P) Repeatedly ask him/her until he/she gives in.

(05E) Offer an exchange of favor.

(06E) Do personal favors for him/her.

(07I) Make him/her feel important.

(08C) Obtain informal support of higher ups.

(09R) Sometimes tell him/her the reasons for making the request.

(10E) Help him/her even in personal matters.

(11E) Remind him/her of past favors you did for him/her.

(12C) Bring some friends along to back your request.

(13I) Even when you know you would not use his/her advice, you consult him/her.

(14P) Repeatedly persuade him/her to comply with your arguments as they are the need of the time.

(15C) Get the support of some higher up to back your request.

(16R) Tell him/her exactly why you need his/her help.

(17I) Use the words that make him/her feel good.

(18C) Get everyone else to agree with you before you make the request.

(19E) Remind him/her how hard you had worked and it would only be fair for him/her to help you now.

(20R) Tell him/her the reasons why your plan is the best.

(21C) Refer the matter to a higher authority if the situation so demands.

(22R) Argue your points logically.

(23E) Offer some personal sacrifice in exchange (e.g., doing part of his/her or others' job, etc.).

(24P) Go on asking persistently till he/she does what you want.

Section VIII—Output

1. (SAT) Please indicate how satisfied you are on a seven-point scale with each of the following aspects of your job. Read each item carefully and the number of your choice in the space provided to the left of the item.

Very dissatisfied	1
Dissatisfied	2
Slightly dissatisfied	3
Neutral	4
Slightly satisfied	5
Satisfied	6
Very satisfied	7

HOW SATISFIED ARE YOU WITH...

— (01E) The respect you receive from the people you work with.
— (02E) The amount of job security you have.
— (03I) The chances for advancement on your job.
— (04I) The feeling of worthwhile accomplishment you get from doing your job.
— (05I) The amount of challenge in your job.
— (06E) The friendliness of the people you work with.
— (07I) The amount of personal growth and development you get in doing your job.

2. (COM) Listed below are a series of statements that represent possible feelings that individuals might have for organizations for which they work. With respect to your own feelings about the particular organization for which you are now working, please indicate the degree of your agreement or disagreement with each statement.

Write the number of your choice in the blank beside each statement, based on the following scale.

Strongly disagree	1
Moderately disagree	2
Slightly disagree	3
Neither agree nor disagree	4
Slightly agree	5
Moderately agree	6
Strongly agree	7

(1) I am willing to put in a great deal of effort beyond that normally expected in order to help this organization be successful.
(2) I talk about this organization to my friends as a great organization to work for.

(3) I would accept almost any type of job assignment in order to keep working for this organization.
(4) I find that my values and the organization's values are very similar.
(5) I am proud to tell others that I am a part of this organization.
(6) I could just as well be working for a different organization as long as the type of work was similar.
(7) This organization really inspires the very best in me in the way of job performance.
(8) Often, I find it difficult to agree with this organization's policies on important matters relating to its employees.
(9) I really care about the fate of this organization.

3. (EF) Every worker produces something in his/her work. It may be a 'product' or a 'service.' We would like you to think carefully of the things that you produce in your work and of the things produced by those people who work around you in your division.

1. Thinking now of the various things produced by the people you know in your division, how much are they producing? CHECK ONE:
   1. Their production is very high.
   2. It is fairly high.
   3. It is neither high nor low.
   4. It is fairly low.
   5. It is very low.

2. How good would you say is the quality of the products or service produced by the people you know in your division? CHECK ONE:
   1. Their products or services are of excellent quality.
   2. Good quality.
   3. Fair quality.
   4. Their quality is not too good.
   5. Their quality is poor.

3. Do the people in your division seem to get maximum output from the resources (money, people, equipment, etc.) they have available? That is, how efficiently do they do their work? CHECK ONE:
   1. They do not work efficiently at all.
   2. Not too efficient.
   3. Fairly efficient.
   4. They are very efficient.
   5. They are extremely efficient.

4. How good a job is done by the people in your division in anticipating problems that may come up in the future and preventing them from occurring or minimizing their effects? CHECK ONE:

1. They do an excellent job in anticipating problems.
2. They do a very good job.
3. A fair job.
4. Not too good a job.
5. They do a poor job in anticipating problems.

5. From time to time newer ways are discovered to organize work, and newer equipment and techniques are found with which to do the work. How good a job do the people in your division do at keeping up with these changes that could affect the way they do their work? CHECK ONE:
   1. They do a poor job of keeping up-to-date.
   2. Not too good a job.
   3. A fair job.
   4. They do a good job.
   5. They do an excellent job of keeping up-to-date.

6. When changes are made in the routines or equipment, how quickly do the people in your division accept and adjust to these changes? CHECK ONE:
   1. Most people accept and adjust to them immediately.
   2. They adjust very rapidly, but not immediately.
   3. Fairly rapidly.
   4. Rather slowly.
   5. Most people accept and adjust to them very slowly.

7. What proportion of the people in your division readily accept and adjust to these changes? CHECK ONE:
   1. Considerably less than half of the people accept and adjust to these changes readily.
   2. Slightly less than half do.
   3. The majority do.
   4. Considerably more than half do.
   5. Practically everyone accepts and adjusts to those changes readily.

8. From time to time emergencies arise, such as crash programs, schedules moved ahead, or a breakdown in the flow of work. When these emergencies occur, they cause work overloads for many people. Some work-groups cope with these emergencies more readily and successfully than others. How good a job do the people in your division do at coping with these situations? CHECK ONE:
   1. They do a poor job of handling emergency situations.
   2. They do not do very well.

3. They do a fair job.
4. They do a good job.
5. They do an excellent job of handling these situations.

Once again thank you for your help!

◄ Appendix III ►

An Illustration of Waba

An Illustration

Table 1 shows a reduction of data into total, within, and between cell components. As mentioned earlier, the variable A under consideration is the leader behavior of three leaders when each one of them evaluates his or her behavior towards three subordinates each. Table 1 also shows the calculation of η_{BA}, η_{WA}, and η_{BWA} (equals 0).

Table 2 shows the inferences drawn from these mathematical indicators and their levels of significance.

Table 1

An Illustration of Within-and-Between Analysis (WABA) of Leader Behavior (Variable A).

	Cell I			Cell II			Cell III			SUMMATION	
	a	b	c	d	e	f	g	h	i	Numerical	
Variable A											
Scores (A)	1	9	5	6	2	1	8	1	3	36	$\Sigma(A)$
Average ($\bar{A}$)	4	4	4	4	4	4	4	4	4	36	$\Sigma(\bar{A})$
Cell Averages ($\bar{A}j$)	5	5	5	3	3	3	4	4	4	36	$\Sigma(\bar{A}j)$
Total Deviations (A − $\bar{A}$)	−3	5	1	2	−2	−3	4	−3	−1	00	$\Sigma(A - \bar{A}) = 0$
Within Cell Deviations (A − $\bar{A}j$)	−4	4	0	3	−1	−2	4	−3	−1	00	$\Sigma(A - \bar{A}j) = 0$
Between Cell Deviations ($\bar{A}j$ − $\bar{A}$)	−1	−1	−1	1	1	1	0	0	0	00	$\Sigma(\bar{A}j - \bar{A}) = 0$
Squared Total Deviations (A − $\bar{A}$)²	9	25	1	4	4	9	16	9	1	78	$\Sigma(A - \bar{A})^2$
Squared Within Deviations (A − $\bar{A}j$)²	16	16	0	9	1	4	16	9	0	72	$\Sigma(A - \bar{A}j)^2$
Squared Between Deviations ($\bar{A}j$ − $\bar{A}$)²	1	1	1	1	1	1	0	0	0	6	$\Sigma(\bar{A}j - \bar{A})^2$
Cross Products for Variable A											
Total by Between	3	−5	−1	2	−2	−3	0	0	0	−6	$\Sigma(A - \bar{A})(\bar{A}j - \bar{A})$ $(A - \bar{A})(\bar{A}j - \bar{A})$
Total by Within	12	20	0	6	2	6	16	9	1	72	$\Sigma(A - \bar{A})(A - \bar{A}j)$ $(A - \bar{A})(A - \bar{A}j)$
Between by Within	4	−4	0	3	−1	−2	0	0	0	0	$\Sigma(\bar{A}j - \bar{A})(A - \bar{A}j)$ $(\bar{A}j - \bar{A})(A - \bar{A}j)$

Table 1 continued

Table 1 continued

Calculations for Variable A

Between eta correlations (η_{BA}) $= \left[\dfrac{\Sigma (A - \overline{A})(\overline{A}j - \overline{A})}{\sqrt{\Sigma (A - \overline{A})^2 \, \Sigma (\overline{A}j - \overline{A})^2}} \right]$

$= -6 / \sqrt{(78)(6)}$

$= .28$

Within eta correlations (η_{WA}) $= \left[\dfrac{\Sigma (A - \overline{A})(A - \overline{A}j)}{\sqrt{\Sigma (A - \overline{A})^2 \, \Sigma (A - \overline{A}j)^2}} \right]$

$= 72 / \sqrt{(78)(72)}$

$= .96$

Between with Within Correlations (η_{BWA}) $= \left[\dfrac{\Sigma (\overline{A}j - \overline{A})(A - \overline{A}j)}{\sqrt{\Sigma (A - \overline{A})^2 \, \Sigma (A - \overline{A}j)^2}} \right]$

$= 0 / \sqrt{(6)(72)}$

$= 0$

Table 2
Inferences from WABA for Variable A

	Variable A	
eta between (2)	.28	
eta within (6)	.96	
E ratio	.29	
F ratio	.25	
Inferences		
Wholes:		
15° E ≥ 1.30		
30° E ≥ 1.73		
.05 F ≥ 5.14		
.01 F ≥ 10.92		
Parts:		
15° E ≥ .77		#
30° E ≥ .58		#
.05 F ≤ .05		
.01 F ≤ .01		
Reject:		
15 E (all others)		
30 E (all others)		
.05 F (all others)		#
.01 F (all others)		#

Note: # shows the location of data (level); numbers in parantheses are the degrees of freedom.

References

Allen, R.W., Madison, D.L., Porter, L.W., Renwick, P.A., & Mayes, B.T. (1979). Organizational politics: Tactics and characteristics of its actors. *California Management Review, 22,* 77–83.

Allport, F.H. (1954). The structuring of events: Outline of general theory with applications to psychology. *Psychological Review, 61,* 281–303.

Allport, F.H. (1967). A theory of enestruence (event structure theory): Report of progress. *American Psychologist, 22,* 1–24.

Altman, I., & Taylor, D.A. (1973). *Social penetration: The development of interpersonal relationships.* New York: Holt, Rinehart, Winston.

Andrews, J.D.W. (1967). The achievement motive and advancement in two types of organizations. *Journal of Personality and Social Psychology, 6,* 163–168.

Ansari, M.A. (1980). Organizational climate: Homogeneity within and heterogeneity between organizations. *Journal of Social and Economic Studies, 8,* 89–96.

Ansari, M.A. (1987). Effects of leader persistence and leader behavior on leadership perceptions. *Pakistan Journal of Psychological Research, 2,* 1–10.

Ansari, M.A. (1990). *Managing people at work.* New Delhi: Sage Publications.

Ansari, M.A., & Kapoor, A. (1987). Organizational context and upward influence tactics. *Organizational Behavior and Human Decision Processes, 40,* 39–49.

Ansari, M.A., Baumgartel, H., & Sullivan, G. (1982). The personal orientation-organizational climate *fit* and managerial success. *Human Relations, 35,* 1159–1178.

Ansari, M.A., Kapoor, A., & Rehana (1984). Social power in Indian organizations. *Indian Journal of Industrial Relations, 20,* 237–244.

Ansari, M.A., Tandon, K., & Lakhtakia, U. (1989). Organizational context and leader's use of influence strategies. *Psychological Studies, 34,* 29–38.

Argyle, M., Gardner, G., & Ciofi, F. (1958). Supervisory methods related to productivity, absenteeism, and labor turnover. *Human Relations, 11,* 23–40.

Atkinson, J.W. (1964). *An introduction to motivation.* Princeton, NJ: D. Van Nostrand Company.

Bachman, J.G., Bowers, D.G., & Marcus, P.M. (1968). Bases of supervisory power: A comparative study in five organizational settings. In A.S. Tannenbaum (Ed.), *Control in organizations* (pp. 213–227). New York: McGraw-Hill.

Baker, D.D., & Ganster, D.C. (1985). Leader communication style: A test of average versus vertical dyad linkage models. *Group and Organization Studies, 10,* 242–259.

Barnard, C.I. (1938). *The functions of the executive.* Cambridge, MA: Harvard University Press.

Bass, B.M. (1960). *Leadership, psychology and organizational behavior.* New York: Harper.

Bass, B.M. (1975). *Exercise supervise.* Scotsville, NY: Trasnational Programs.

Bass, B.M. (1980). Team productivity and individual member competence. *Small Group Behavior, 11,* 431–504.

Bass, B.M. (1981). *Stogdill's handbook of leadership.* New York: Free Press.

Bass, B.M., & Ryterband, E.C. (1979). *Organizational psychology* (2nd ed.). Boston, MA: Allyn & Bacon.

Baumgartel, H. (1981). Human factors in the transfer of technology in national development. *Human Futures, 4,* 1–9.

Bennis, W.G. (1966). The decline of bureaucracy and organization of the future. In W.G. Bennis (Ed.), *Changing organizations* (pp. 3–15). New York: McGraw-Hill.

Bernard, L.L. (1926). *An introduction to social psychology.* New York: Holt, Rinehart, Winston.

Bhal, K.T., & Ansari, M.A. (1996). Measuring quality of interaction between leaders and members. *Journal of Applied Social Psychology, 26,* 945–972.

Bierstedt, P. (1950). An analysis of social power. *American Sociological Review, 15,* 730–738.

Birsch, D., & Veroff, J. (1966). *Motivation: A study of action.* Monterey, CA: Brooks/Cole.

Blake, R.R., & Mouton, J.S. (1962). The intergroup dynamics of win-lose conflict and problem-solving collaboration in union-management relations. In M. Sherif (Ed.), *Intergroup relations and leadership.* New York: Wiley.

Blake, R.R., & Mouton, J.S. (1964). *The managerial grid.* Houston, TX: Gulf Publishing Company.

Blau, P.M. (1964). *Exchange and power in social life.* New York: Wiley.

Bowers, K.S. (1973). Situationism in psychology: An analysis and critique. *Psychological Bulletin, 80,* 307–336.

Bruning, N.S., & Cashman, J.F. (1978). Initializing the linkage process: A longitudinal study of attitudes, attraction, and leadership dynamics. In D.F. Ray & T.B. Green (Eds.), *Toward a renewal in management thought and practice* (pp. 86–88). Missisippi: Mississippi State University Press.

Burns, J.M. (1978). *Leadership.* New York: Harper & Row.

Byrd, C. (1940). *Social psychology.* New York: Appleton-Century-Crofts.

Cartwright, D. (1959). A field theoretical conception of power. In D. Cartwright (Ed.), *Studies in social power* (pp. 183–220). Ann Arbor, MI: Institute for Social Research.

Cartwright, D. (1965). Influence, leadership, control. In J.G. March (Ed.), *Handbook of organizations* (pp. 1–47). Chicago, IL: Rand McNally.

Cashman, J., Dansereau, F., Graen, G., & Haga, W. (1976). Organizational understructure and leadership: A longitudinal investigation of the managerial role-making process. *Organizational Behaviour and Human Performance, 15,* 278–296.

Chattopadhyay, G.P. (1975). Dependence in Indian culture: From mud huts to company board rooms. *Economic and Political Weekly, 10,* 30–38.

Chibber, M.L. (1995). *Sai Baba's Mahavakya on Leadership.* Faber, VA: Leela Press.

Crouch, A., & Yetton, P. (1988). Manager-subordinate dyads: Relationships among task and social contact, manager friendliness and subordinate performance in management groups. *Organizational Behavior and Human Decision Processes, 41,* 65–82.

Daftuar, C.N., & Krishna, K.P. (1971). Perceived characteristics of good and bad supervisors by white collared bank employees. *Indian Journal of Psychology, 46,* 45–53.

Dahl, R.A. (1957). The concept of power. *Behavioral Science, 2,* 201–218.

Dansereau, F., & Dumas, M. (1977). Pratfalls and pitfalls in drawing inferences about leader behavior in organizations. In J. Hunt & L. Larson (Eds.), *Leadership: The cutting edge* (pp. 68–83). Carbondale, IL: Southern Illinois University Press.

Dansereau, F., Alutto, J.A., & Yammarino, F.J. (1984). *Theory testing in organizational behavior: The varient approach.* Englewood Cliffs, NJ: Prentice-Hall.

Dansereau, F., Cashman, J., & Graen, G. (1973). Instrumentality theory and equity theory as complementary approaches in predicting relationship of leadership and turnover among managers. *Organizational Behaviour and Human Performance, 10,* 184–200.

Dansereau, F., Graen, G., & Haga, W.J. (1975). A vertical dyad linkage approach to leadership within formal organizations. *Organizational Behavior and Human Performance, 13,* 46–78.

Dansereau, F., Alutto, J.A., Markham, S.E., & Dumas, M. (1982). Multiplexed supervision and leadership: An application of within and between analysis. In J.G. Hunt, U. Sekaran, & C.A. Schriesheim (Eds.), *Leadership: Beyond establishment views* (pp. 81–103). Carbondale, IL: Southern Illinois University Press.

De, N.R. (1974). Conditions for work culture. *Indian Journal of Industrial Relations, 9,* 587–598.

Dienesch, R.M., & Liden, R.C. (1986). Leader-member exchange model of leadership: A critique and further development. *Academy of Management Review, 11,* 618–634.

Dockery, T.M., & Steiner, D.D. (1990). The role of the initial interaction in leader-member exchange. *Group and Organization Studies, 15,* 395–413.

Duarte, N.T., Goodson, J.R., & Klich, N.R. (1994). Effects of dyadic quality and duration on performance appraisal. *Academy of Management Journal, 37,* 499–521.

Duchon, D., Green, S.G., & Taber, T.D. (1986). Vertical dyad linkage: A longitudinal assessment of antecedents, measures, and consequences. *Journal of Applied Psychology, 71,* 56–60.

Dunnette, M.D. (1972). Research needs of the future in industrial and organizational psychology. *Personnel Psychology, 25,* 31–40.

Emerson, R.M. (1962). Power-dependence relations. *American Sociological Review, 27,* 31–41.

Etzioni, A. (1975). *Comparative Analysis of Complex Organizations.* New York: Free Press.

Evans, M.G. (1970). The effects of supervisory behavior on the path-goal relationship. *Organizational Behavior and Human Performance, 5,* 277–298.

Falbo, T. (1977). Multidimensional scaling of power strategies. *Journal of Personality and Social Psychology, 35*, 537–547.

Falbo, T. (1982). PAQ styles and power strategies used in intimate relationships. *Psychology of Women Quarterly, 6*, 399–405.

Falbo, T., & Peplau, L.A. (1980). Power strategies in intimate relationships. *Journal of Personality and Social Psychology, 38*, 618–628.

Farrow, D.L., Valenzi, E.R., & Bass, B.M. (1980). A comparison of leadership and situational characteristics within profit and non-profit organizations. *Proceedings of the Academy of Management.*

Ferrel, D.C., & Peterson, J.C. (1982). Patterns of political behavior in organizations. *Academy of Management Review, 7*, 403–412.

Ferris, G.R. (1985). Role of leadership in the employee withdrawal process: A constructive replication. *Journal of Applied Psychology, 70*, 777–781.

Fiedler, F.E. (1973). *A theory of leadership effectiveness.* New York: McGraw-Hill.

Fiedler, F.E. (1978). The contingency model and the dynamics of the leadership process. *Advances in Experimental Social Psychology, 15*, 59–112.

Fisher, R.A. (1915). Frequency distribution of the values of the correlation coefficient in samples from an indefinitely large population. *Biometrika, 10*, 507–521.

Fleishman, E.A. (1953). The description of supervisory behavior. *Personnel Psychology, 37*, 1–6.

Fleishman, E.A. (1957). A leader behavior description for industry. In R.M. Stogdill & A.E. Coons (Eds.), *Leader behavior: Its description and measurement.* Columbus, OH: Bureau of Business Research, Ohio State University.

Fleishman, E.A., & Harris, E.F. (1962). Patterns of leadership behavior related to employee grievances and turnover. *Personnel Psychology, 15*, 43–56.

Fleishman, E.A., & Simmons, J. (1970). Relationship between leadership patterns and effectiveness ratings among Israeli foremen. *Personnel Psychology, 23*, 169–172.

French, J.R.P., & Raven, B. (1959). The bases of social power. In D. Cartwright (Ed.), *Studies in social power* (pp. 118–149). Ann Arbor, MI: Institute for Social Research.

Fujii, D.S. (1977). A dyadic interactive approach to the study of leader behaviors. *Dissertation Abstracts International, 37*, 5415–5416.

Goodchilds, J.C., Quadrado, C., & Raven, B.H. (1975, April). Getting one's way: Self reported influence strategies. Paper presented at the meeting of the Western Psychological Association, Sacramento, California.

Goodstein, L.D. (1981). Getting your way: A training activity in understanding power and influence. *Group and Organization Studies, 6*, 283–290.

Graen, G. (1976). Role making processes within complex organizations. In M.D. Dunnette (Ed.), *Handbook of industrial and organizational psychology* (pp. 1201–1245). Chicago, IL: Rand McNally.

Graen, G., & Cashman, J. (1975). A role-making model of leadership in formal organizations: A developmental approach. In J.G. Hunt & L.L. Larson (Eds.), *Leadership frontiers* (pp. 143–165). Kent, OH: Kent State University Press.

Graen, G., & Ginsburgh, S. (1977). Job resignation as a function of role orientation and leader acceptance: A longitudinal investigation of organizational assimilation. *Organizational Behavior and Human Performance, 19*, 1–17.

Graen, G.B., & Scandura, T.A. (1987). Toward a psychology of dyadic organizing. *Research in Organizational Behavior, 9*, 175–208.

Graen, G., & Schiemann, W. (1978). Leader-member agreement: A vertical dyad linkage approach. *Journal of Applied Psychology, 63*, 206–212.

Graen, G., Cashman, J., Ginsburgh, S., & Schiemann, W. (1977). Effects of linking pin quality on the quality of working life of lower participants. *Administrative Science Quarterly, 22*, 491–504.

Graen, G., Dansereau, F., & Minami, T. (1972a). Dysfunctional leadership styles. *Organizational Behavior and Human Performance, 7*, 216–236.

Graen, G., Dansereau, F., & Minami, T. (1972b). An empirical test of the man-in-the middle hypothesis among executives in a hierachical organization employing a unit-set analysis. *Organizational Behavior and Human Performance, 8*, 262–285.

Graen, G., Liden, R., & Hoel, W. (1982). Role of leadership in the employee withdrawal process. *Journal of Applied Psychology, 67*, 868–872.

Graen, G., Novak, M., & Sommerkamp, P. (1982). The effects of leader-member exchange and job design on productivity and satisfaction: Testing a dual attachment model. *Organizational Behavior and Human Performance, 30*, 109–131.

Graen, G., Orris, J.B., & Johnson, T. (1973). Role assimilation processes in a complex organization. *Journal of Vocational Behavior, 3*, 395–420.

Greene, C.N. (1979). Questions of causation in the path-goal theory of leadership. *Academy of Management Journal, 22*, 22–41.

Greenwald, A.G. (1975). Consequence of prejudice against the null hypothesis. *Psychological Bulletin, 82*, 1–20.

Grosser, D., Polansky, N., & Lippitt, R. (1951). A laboratory study of behavioral contagion. *Human Relations, 4*, 115–142.

Guion, R.M. (1973). A note on organizational climate. *Organizational Behavior and Human Performance, 9*, 120–125.

Haga, W.J., Graen, G.B., & Dansereau, F. (1974). Professionalism and role making in a service organization: A longitudinal investigation. *American Sociological Review, 39*, 122–133.

Halpin, A.W., & Winer, B.J. (1957). A factorial study of the leader behavior descriptions. In R.M. Stogdill & A.E. Coons (Eds.), *Leader behavior: Its description and measurement* (pp. 39–52), Columbus, OH: Bureau of Business Research, Ohio State University.

Hackman, J.R., & Oldham, G.R. (1976). Motivation through the design of work: Test of a theory. *Organizational Behavior and Human Performance, 16*, 250–279.

Hannan, M.T. (1971). *Aggregation and disaggregation in sociology.* Lexington, MA: Heath-Lexington.

Hellreigel, D., & Slocum, J.W. (1974). Organizational climate: Measures, research and contingencies. *Academy of Management Journal, 17*, 255–280.

Hemphill, J.K. (1949). The Leader and his group. *Journal of Educational Research, 28*, 225–229.

Hemphill, J.K. (1950). *Leader behavior description.* Columbus, OH: Bureau of Educational Research, Ohio State University.

Hemphill, J.K., & Coons, A.E. (1957). Development of the leader behavior description questionnaire. In R.M. Stogdill & A.E. Coons (Eds.), *Leader behavior: Its description and measurement* (pp. 6–38). Columbus, OH: Bureau of Business Research, Ohio State University.

Herold, D. (1977). Two-way influence processes in leader-follower dyads. *Academy of Management Journal, 20,* 224–237.

Hersey, P., & Blanchard, K. (1982). *Management of organizational behavior* (4th ed.). Englewood Cliffs, NJ: Prentice-Hall.

Hersey P., Blanchard, K.H., & Natemeyer, W.E. (1979). *Situational leadership, perception and the impact of power.* Centre for leadership studies.

Hofstede, G. (1980). *Culture's consequences.* Beverley Hills, CA: Sage Publications.

Hollander, E.P. (1960). Competence and conformity in the acceptance of influence. *Journal of Abnormal and Social Psychology, 61,* 361–365.

Hollander, E.P. (1961). Some effects of perceived status on responses to innovative behavior. *Journal of Abnormal and Social Psychology, 63,* 247–250.

Hollander, E.P. (1976). *Emergent leadership and social influence.* St. Louis, MO: University of Washington Press.

Homans, G.C. (1951). *The human group.* New York: Harcourt, Brace.

Homans, G.C. (1961). *Social behavior: Its elementary form.* New York: Harcourt, Brace, & World.

House, R.J., & Filley, A.C. (1971). Leadership style, hierarchical influence, and satisfaction of subordinate role expectations: A test of Likert's proposition. *Journal of Applied Psychology, 55,* 422–432.

Hundal, P.S. (1971). A study of enterpreneurial motivation: Comparison of fast and slow progressing small scale industrial entrepreneurs in Punjab, India. *Journal of Applied Psychology, 55,* 317–323.

Hunt, J.G., Osborn, R.M., & Larson, L.L. (1975). Upper level technical orientation of first level leadership within a noncontingency and contingency framework. *Academy of Management Journal, 18,* 475–488.

Indik, B.P. (1968). The scope of the problem and some suggestions toward a solution. In B.P. Indik & F.K. Berrien (Eds.), *People, groups and organizations* (pp. 3–10). New York: Teachers college Press.

Jacobs, T.O. (1970). *Leadership and exchange in formal organizations.* Alexandria, VA: Human Resources Research Organization.

James, L.R., & Jones, A.P. (1974). Organizational climate: A review of theory and research, *Psychological Bulletin, 81,* 1096–1112.

Janda, K.J. (1960). Towards the explication of leadership in terms of the concept of power. *Human Relations, 13,* 345–363.

Johnson, T.W., & Graen, G. (1973). Organizational assimilation and role rejection. *Organizational Behavior and Human Performance, 10,* 72–87.

Jones, A.P., & James, L.R. (1979). Psychological climate: Dimensions and relationships of individual and aggregated work environment perceptions. *Organizational Behavior and Human Performance, 23,* 201–250.

Kahn, R.L., & Katz, D. (1953). Leadership practices in relation to productivity and morale. In D. Cartwright & A. Zander (Eds.), *Group dynamics.* New York: Harper & Row.

Kahn, R.L., & Tannenbaum, A.S. (1957). Leadership practices and member participation in local unions. *Personnel Psychology, 10,* 277–292.

Kahn, R.L., Wolfe, D.M., Quinn, R.P., Snoek, J.D., & Rosenthal, R.A. (1964). *Organizational stress.* New York: Wiley.

Kakar, S. (1971). Authority patterns of subordinate behavior in Indian organizations. *Administrative Science Quarterly, 16,* 298–307.

Kapoor, A. (1987). Some of the determinants of intraorganizational influence strategies. Unpublished doctoral dissertation, Kanpur, India: Indian Institute of Technology.

Katerberg, R., & Hom, P.W. (1981). Effects of within-group and between-groups variation in leadership. *Journal of Applied Psychology, 66,* 218–223.

Katz, D., & Kahn, R.L. (1978). *The social psychology of organizations.* New York: Wiley.

Katz, D., Maccoby, N., & Morse N. (1950). *Productivity, supervision and Morale in an office situation.* Ann Arbor, MI: Institute for Social Research, University of Michigan.

Khandwalla, P.N. (1977). *The design of organizations.* New York: Harcourt, Brace, Jovanovich.

Kim, K.I., & Organ, D.W. (1982). Determinants of leader-subordinate exchange relationships. *Group and Organization Studies, 7,* 77–89.

Kipnis, D. (1958). The effects of leadership style and leadership power upon the inducement of an attitude change. *Journal of Abnormal and Social Psychology, 57,* 173–180.

Kipnis, D. (1976). *The power holders.* Chicago, IL: University of Chicago Press.

Kipnis, D., & Schmidt, S. (1983). An influence perspective on bargaining. In M. Bazerman & R. Lewicki (Eds.), *Negotiating in organizations.* Beverly Hills, CA: Sage.

Kipnis, D., & Vanderveer, R. (1971). Ingratiation and the use of power. *Journal of Personality and Social Psychology, 17,* 280–286.

Kipnis, D., Cohn, E., & Schwarz, L. (1976, November). The measurement of influence among dating couples. Paper presented at the meeting of the American Institute for Decision Sciences, San Fransisco.

Kipnis, D., Schmidt, S.M., & Wilkinson, I. (1980). Intraorganizational influence tactics: Explorations in getting one's way. *Journal of Applied Psychology, 65,* 440–452.

Kipnis, D., Schmidt, S., Price, K., & Stitt, C. (1981). Why do I like thee: Is it your performance or my orders? *Journal of Applied Psychology, 66,* 324–328.

Kirk, R.E. (1968). *Experimental design.* Belmont, CA: Brooks/Cole.

Kochan, T.A. (1975). Determinants of the power of boundary units in an interorganizational bargaining relation. *Administrative Science Quarterly, 20,* 434–452.

Kochan, T.A., Schmidt, S.M., & de Cotiis, T.A. (1975). Superior-subordinate relations: Leadership and headship. *Human Relations, 28,* 279–294.

Kozlowski, S.W.J., & Doherty, M.L. (1989). Integration of climate and leadership: Examination of a neglected issue. *Journal of Applied Psychology, 74,* 546–553.

Krackhardt, D., Mckenna, J., Porter, L.W., & Steers, R.M. (1981). Supervisory behavior and employee turnover: A field experiment. *Academy of Management Journal, 24,* 249–259.

Kumar, U., & Singh, K.K. (1976). The interpersonal construct system of the Indian manager: A determinant of organizational behavior. *Indian Journal of Psychology, 51,* 275–290.

Lakhtakia, U. (1990). Managing conflict at the interpersonal level: A study of some antecedents. Unpublished doctoral dissertation. Kanpur, India: Indian Institute of Technology.

Lawrence, L.C., & Smith, P.C. (1955). Group decision and employee participation. *Journal of Applied Psychology, 39*, 334–337.

Lawshe, C.H., & Nagle, B.F. (1953). Productivity and attitude toward supervisor. *Journal of Applied Psychology, 37*, 159–162.

Levinger, G., & Snoek, J.D. (1972). *Attraction in relationship: A new look at interpersonal attraction*. Morristown, NJ: General Learning Press.

Lewin, K. (1951). *Field theory in social sciences*. New York: Harper.

Lewin, K., Lippitt, R., & White, R.K. (1939). Patterns of aggressive behavior in experimentally created social climates. *Journal of Social Psychology, 10*, 271–299.

Liden, R.C., Sparrowe, R.T., & Wayne, S.J. (1997). Leader-member exchange theory. The past and potential for the future. In G.R. Ferris (Ed.) *Research in Personnel and Human Resource Management, 15*, (pp. 47–119). Greenwich, C.T.: JAI Press.

Liden, R.C., Wayne, S.R., & Stilwell, D. (1993). A longitudinal study on the early development of leader-member exchanges. *Journal of Applied Psychology, 78*, 662–674.

Likert, R. (1959). Motivational approach to management development. *Harvard Business Review, 37*, 75–82.

Likert, R. (1961). *New patterns of management*. New York: McGraw-Hill.

Likert, R. (1967). *The human organization: Its management and value*. New York: McGraw-Hill.

Litwin, G.H. (1968). Climate and motivation: An experimental study. In R. Tagiuri & G.H. Litwin (Eds.), *Organizational climate*. Boston, MA: Harvard University, Graduate School of Business Administration.

Litwin, G.H., & Stringer, R.A. (1968). *Motivation and organizational climate*. Boston: Harvard University, Graduate School of Business Administration.

Lowin, A., & Craig, J. (1968). The influence of level of performance on managerial style: An experimental object-lesson in the ambiguity of correlational data. *Organizational Behavior and Human Performance, 3*, 441–458.

Major, D.A., Kozlowski, S.W., Chao, G.T., & Gardner, P.D. (1995). A longitudinal investigation of newcomer expectations, early socialisation outcomes and moderating effects of role development factors. *Journal of Applied Psychology, 78*, 662–674.

Mann, F.C., & Hoffman, L.R. (1960). *Automation and the worker: A study of social change in power plants*. New York: Holt, Rinehart, Winston.

March, J.G. (1955). An introduction to the theory and measurement of influence. *American Political Science Review, 49*, 431–451.

Markham, S., Dansereau, F., & Alutto, J. (1979). *Fundamental problems in leadership research*. In E.L. Miller (ed.), Proceedings of the 22nd annual conference of the midwest academy of management (pp. 404–412). Ann Arbor, MI: Division of Research, Graduate School of Business Administration, University of Michigan.

Martin, T.N., & Hunt, J.G. (1980). Social influence and intent to leave: A path-analytic process model. *Personnel Psychology, 33*, 505–528.

Mayes, B.T., & Ganster, D.C. (1982). Politics and turnover: A test of hypotheses based on fight/flight responses to job stress. Unpublished manuscript, Lincoln, NE: University of Nebraska.

McClelland, D.C. (1961). *The achieving society*. Princeton, NJ: D. Van Nostrand Company.

McClelland, D.C. (1970). The two faces of power. *Journal of International Affairs, 24,* 29–47.

McClelland, D.C. (1975). *Power: The inner experience.* New York: Irvington.

McClelland, D.C. (1976). Power is the great motivator. *Harvard Business Review, 54,* 100–110.

McClelland, D.C., & Winter, D.G. (1969). *Motivating economic achievement.* New York: Free Press.

McClelland, D.C., Atkinson, J.W., Clark, R.A., & Lowell, E.L. (1953). *The achievement motive.* New York: Appleton-Century-Crofts.

McGregor, D. (1960). *The human side of enterprise.* New York: McGraw-Hill.

Mechanic, D. (1962). Sources of power of lower participants in complex organizations. *Administrative Science Quarterly, 7,* 349–364.

Merton, R. (1957). *Social theory and social structure.* Glencoe, IL: Free Press.

Meyer, H.H., & Walker, W.B. (1961). Need for achievement and risk preferences as they relate to attitudes toward reward systems and performance appraisal in an industrial setting. *Journal of Applied Psychology, 45,* 251–256.

Miner, J.B. (1980). *Theories of organizational behavior.* Hinsdale, IL: Dryden Press.

Minton, H.L. (1967). Power as a personality construct. In B.A. Maher (Ed.), *Progress in experimental personality research 4,* (pp. 229–267). New York: Academic Press.

Mitchell, T.R. (1979). Organizational behavior. *Annual Review of Psychology, 30,* 243–281.

Mobley, W.H. (1977). Intermediate linkages in the relationship between job satisfaction and employee turnover. *Journal of Applied Psychology, 62,* 237–240.

Mobley, W.H., Griffeth, R.W., Hand, H.H., & Meglino, B. (1979). Review and conceptual analysis of the employee turnover process. *Psychological Bulletin, 86,* 493–522.

Mott, P.E. (1972). *Characteristics of effective organizations.* New York: Harper & Row.

Mowday, R.T. (1978). The exercise of upward influence in organizations. *Administrative Science Quarterly, 23,* 137–156.

Mulder, M., Binkhorst., & Van Oers, T. (1983). Systematic appraisal of leadership effectiveness of consultants. *Human Relations, 36,* 1045–1064.

Mulder, M., de Jong, R.D., Koppelaar, L., & Verhage, J. (1977). *Power, situation and leader's effectiveness—An organizational field study by means of the Influence Analysis questionnaire.* Inter-university Foundation for Business Administration at Delft, the Department of Clinical Psychology, Utrecht University, and the Department of Social Psychology, Free University, Amsterdam.

Murray, H.A. (1938). *Explorations in Personality.* New York: Oxford University Press.

Nachman, S., Dansereau, F., & Naughton, T.J. (1983). Negotiating latitude: A within-and between-groups analysis of a key construct in the vertical dyad linkage theory of leadership. *Psychological Reports, 53,* 171–177.

Nachman, S., Dansereau, F., & Naughton, T.J. (1985). Levels of analysis and the vertical dyad linkage approach to leadership. *Psychological Reports, 57,* 661–662.

Nie, N.H., Hull, C.H., Jenkins, J.G., Steinbrenner, K., & Bent, D. (1975). *SPSS: Statistical package for the social sciences.* New York: McGraw-Hill.

Nunnally, J.C. (1978). *Psychometric theory.* New York: McGraw-Hill.

Pandey, J. (1976). Effect of leadership style, personality characteristics and method of leader selection on member's and leader's behavior. *European Journal of Social Psychology, 6,* 475–489.

Parsons, T. (1956). The relation between the small group and the larger social system. In R. Grinker (Ed.), *Toward a unified theory of behavior.* New York: Basic Books.

Patchen, M. (1962). Supervisory methods and group performance norms. *Administrative Science Quarterly, 7,* 275–294.

Patchen, M. (1974). The locus and basis of influence in organizational decisions. *Organizational Behavior and Human Performance, 11,* 195–221.

Payne, R.L., & Pugh, D.S. (1976). Organizational structure and climate. In M.D. Dunnette (Ed.), *Handbook of industrial and organizational psychology.* Chicago, IL: Rand McNally.

Peabody, R.L. (1962). Perceptions of organizational authority: A comparative analysis. *Administrative Science Quarterly, 6,* 463–482.

Pestonjee, D.M. (1973). *Organizational structure and job attitudes.* Calcutta: Minerva Associates.

Peterson, D.R. (1977). A functional approach to the study of person-person interactions. In D. Magnusson & N.S. Endler (Eds.), *Personality at the crossroads: Current issues in interactional psychology* (pp. 305–315). Hillsdale, NJ: Lawrence Erlbaum Associates.

Peterson, D.R. (1979). Assessing interpersonal relationships by means of interaction records. *Behavioral Assessment, 1,* 221–236.

Pfeffer, J., & Salancik, G.R. (1975). Determinants of supervisory behavior: A role set analysis. *Human Relations, 28,* 139–153.

Polansky, N., Lippitt, R., & Redl, F. (1950). An investigation of behavioral contagion in groups. *Human Relations, 3,* 319–348.

Porter, L.W., Allen, R.W., & Angle, H.L. (1981). The politics of upward influence in organizations. In B.M. Staw & L.L. Cummings (eds), *Research in organizational behavior, 3,* (pp. 109–149). Greenwich, CT: JAI Press.

Preston, M.G., & Heintz, R.K. (1949). Effects of participatory *vs* supervisory leadership on group judgment. *Journal of Abnormal and Social Psychology, 44,* 345–355.

Raven, B.H. (1965). Social influence and power. In I.D. Steiner & M. Fishbein (Eds.), *Current studies in social psychology* (pp. 371–382). New York: Holt, Rinehart, Winston.

Raven, B.H., & French, J.R.P. Jr. (1958a). Group support, legitimate power, and social influence. *Journal of Personality, 26,* 400–409.

Raven, B.H., & French, J.R.P. Jr. (1958b). Legitimate power, coercive power, and observability in social influence. *Sociometry, 21,* 83–97.

Raven, B.H., & Kruglanski, A. (1970). Conflict and power. In P. Swingle (Ed.), *The structure of conflict* (pp. 69–109). New York: Academic Press.

Rice, R.W. (1978). Construct validity of the least preferred co-worker score. *Psychological Bulletin, 85,* 1199–1237.

Robinson, W.S. (1950). Ecological correlations and the behavior of individuals. *American Sociological Review, 15,* 351–357.

Roland, A. (1980). *Towards a psycho-analytic psychology of hierarchical relationships in Hindu India.* Indian Psychoanalytic Societies, Bombay.

Roland A. (1984). The self in India and America. In V. Kavolis (Ed.), *In designs of selfhood* (pp. 170–191). NJ: Associated University Press.

Rosse, J.G., & Kraut, A.I. (1983). Reconsidering the vertical dyad linkage model of leadership. *Journal of Occupational Psychology, 53,* 63–71.

Russell, B. (1938). *Power: A new social analysis.* New York: Norton.

Saiyadain, M.S. (1974). Personality predisposition and satisfaction with supervisory style. *Indian Journal of Industrial Relations, 10,* 153–161.

Salancik, G.R., & Pfeffer, J. (1974). The bases and use of power in organizational decisionmaking: The case of a university. *Administrative Science Quarterly, 19,* 453–473.

Scandura, T.A., & Graen, G. (1984). Moderating effects of initial leader-member exchange status on the effects of a leadership intervention. *Journal of Applied Psychology, 69,* 428–436.

Scandura, T.A., Graen, G.B., & Novak, M.A. (1986). When managers decide not to decide autocratically: An investigation of leader-member exchange and decision influence. *Journal of Applied Psychology, 71,* 1–6.

Schein, E. (1980). *Organizational psychology.* Englewood Cliffs, NJ: Prentice-Hall.

Schilit, W.K., & Locke, E.A. (1982). A study of upward influence in organizations. *Administrative Science Quarterly, 27,* 304–316.

Schneider, B. (1975). Organizational climate: An essay. *Personnel Psychology, 28,* 447–449.

Schneider, B. (1983). Interactional psychology and organizational behavior. In L. Cummings & B.M. Staw (Eds.) *Research in organizational behavior, 5,* 1–31. Greenwich, CT: JAI Press.

Schriesheim, C. (1979). The similarity of individual directed and group directed leader behavior descriptions. *Academy of Management Journal, 22,* 345–355.

Schriesheim, C., & Kerr, S. (1977). Theories and measures of leadership: A critical appraisal of current and future directions. In J. Hunt & L. Larson (Eds.), *Leadership: The cutting edge* (pp. 9–44). Carbondale, IL: Southern Illinois University Press.

Schriesheim, C.A., Neider, L.L., Scandura, T.A., & Tepper, B.J. (1992). Development and preliminary validation of a new scale (LMX–6) to measure leader member exchange in organizations. *Educational and Psychological Measurement, 52,* 135–147.

Schultz, D.P. (1982). *Psychology and industry today.* New York: Macmillan.

Schumer, H. (1962). Cohesion and leadership in small groups as related to group productivity. *Dissertation Abstracts, 22,* 3735–3736.

Seeman, M. (1957). A comparison of general and specific leader behavior descriptions. In R.M. Stogdill & E.A. Coons (Eds.), *Leadership behavior: Its description and measurement.* Columbus, OH: Bureau of Business Research, Ohio State University.

Seers, A., & Graen, G. (1984). The dual attachment concept: A longitudinal investigation of the combination of task characteristics and leader-member exchange. *Organizational Behavior and Human Performance, 33,* 283–306.

Sells, S.B. (1963). An interactionist look at the environment. *American Psychologist, 18,* 696–702.

Sells, S.B. (1968). The nature of organizational climate. In R. Tagiuri & G.H. Litwin (Eds.), *Organizational climate: Explortions of a concept.* Boston, MA: Harvard University Press.

Shaw, M.E. (1954). Some effects of unequal distribution of information upon group performance in various communication nets. *Journal of Abnormal and Social Psychology, 49,* 547–553.

Shaw, M.E., & Harkey, B. (1976). Some effects of congruency of member characteristics and group structure upon group behavior. *Journal of Personality and Social Psychology, 34,* 412–418.

Singh, C.B.P. (1985). *Behavioral strategies in power relationships.* Unpublished doctoral dissertation, Patna, India: Patna University.

Singh, A.P., & Pestonjee, D.M. (1974). Supervisory behavior and job satisfaction. *Indian Journal of Industrial Relations, 9,* 407–416.

Sinha, D. (1972). Industrial psychology: A trend report. In S.K. Mitra (Ed.), *A survey of research in psychology* (pp. 175–237). Bombay: Popular Prakashan.

Sinha, J.B.P. (1973). *Development through behavior modification.* Bombay: Allied.

Sinha, J.B.P. (1974). A case of reversal in participative management. *Indian Journal of Industrial Relations, 11,* 179–187.

Sinha, J.B.P. (1980). *The nurturant-task leader: A model of effective executive.* New Delhi: Concept.

Sinha, J.B.P. (1987). *Leader's behavior scale.* Patna: ASSERT.

Sinha, J.B.P. (1990). *Work culture in the Indian context.* New Delhi: Sage Publications.

Sinha, J.B.P., & Sinha, M. (1974). Middle class values in organizational perspective. *Journal of Social and Economic Studies, 1,* 95–114.

Snyder, R.A., & Bruning, N.S. (1985). Quality of vertical dyad linkages: Congruence of supervisor and subordinate competence and role stress as explanatory variables. *Group and Organization Studies, 10,* 81–94.

Sparrowe, R.T. (1994). Empowerment in the hospitality industry: An exploration of antecedents and outcomes. *Hospitality Research Journal, 17,* 51–73.

Sparrowe, R.T., & Liden, R.C. (1997). Process and structure in leader-member exchange. *Academy of Management Review, 22,* 522–552.

Steers, R., & Braunstein, D. (1976). A behaviorally based measure of manifest needs in work settings. *Journal of Vocational Behavior, 9,* 251–266.

Steers, R.M., & Porter, L.W. (1987). *Motivation and Work Behavior.* New York: McGraw-Hill.

Stogdill, R.M. (1948). Personal factors associated with leadership: A survey of the literature. *The Journal of Psychology, 25,* 35–71.

Tandon, K., Ansari, M.A., & Kapoor, A. (1989). Attributing upward influence attempts in organizations. *The Journal of Psychology, 125,* 59–63.

Tannenbaum, R., & Schmidt, W.H. (1958). How to choose a leadership pattern. *Harvard Business Review, 36,* 95–101.

Tead, O. (1935). *The Art of leadership.* New York: McGraw-Hill.

Thibaut, J.W., & Kelley, H.H. (1959). *The social psychology of groups.* New York: Wiley.

Torrance, E.P. (1953). Methods of conducting critiques of group problem-solving performance. *Journal of Appjlied Psychology, 37,* 394–398.

Utecht, R.E., & Heier, W.D. (1976). The contingency model and successful military leadership. *Academy of Management Journal, 19,* 606–618.

Van de Ven, A.H., & Astley, W.G. (1981). A commentary on organizational behavior in the 1980's. *Decision Sciences, 12,* 388–398.

Vecchio, R.P. (1982). A further test of leadership effects due to between-group variation and within-group variation. *Journal of Applied Psychology, 67,* 200–208.

Vecchio, R.P. (1985). Predicting employee turnover from leader-member exchange: A failure to replicate. *Academy of Management Journal, 28,* 478–485.

Vecchio, R., & Gobdel, B. (1984). The vertical dyad linkage model of leadership: Problems and prospects. *Organizational Behavior and Human Performance, 34,* 5–20.

Vecchio, R.P., Griffeth, R.W., & Hom, P.W. (1986). The predictive utility of the vertical dyad linkage approach. *Journal of Social Psychology, 126,* 617–625.

Vroom, V.H. (1960). *Some personality determinants of effects of participation.* Englewood Cliffs, NJ: Prentice-Hall.

Vroom, V.H., & Yetton, P.W. (1973). *Leadership and decision-making.* Pittsburgh, PA: University of Pittsburgh Press.

Wainer, H.A., & Rubin, I.M. (1969). Motivation of research and development enterpreneurs: Determinants of company success. *Journal of Applied Psychology, 53,* 178–184.

Wakabayashi, M., & Graen, G. (1984). The Japanese career progress study: A seven year follow up. *Journal of Applied Psychology, 69,* 603–614.

Wakabayashi, M., Graen, G., Graen, M., & Graen, M. (1988). Japanese management progress: Mobility into middle management. *Journal of Applied Psychology, 73,* 217–227.

Wayne, S.J., & Ferris, G.R. (1990). Influence tactics, affect and exchange quality in supervisor—subordinate interactions: A laboratory experiment and field study. *Journal of Applied Psychology, 75,* 487–499.

Wayne, S.J., & Green, S.A. (1993). The effects of leader-member exchange on employee citizenship and impression management behaviour. *Human Relations, 46,* 1431–1440.

Wayne, S.J., Shore, L.M., & Liden, R.C. (1997). Perceived organizational support and leader-member exchange: A social exchange perspective. *Academy of Management Journal, 40,* 82–111.

Weick, K.E. (1979). *The social psychology of organizing.* Readings, MA: Addison-Wesley.

White, J.D. (1963). Autocratic and democratic leadership and their respective groups' power, hierarchies, and morale. *Dissertation Abstracts, 24,* 602.

Wilhelm, C.C., Herd, A.M., & Steiner, D.D. (1993). Attributional conflict between managers and subordinates: An investigation of leader-member exchange effects. *Journal of Organisational Behaviour, 14,* 531–544.

Wilkinson, I., & Kipnis, D. (1978). Interfirm use of power. *Journal of Applied Psychology, 63,* 315–320.

Winer, B.J. (1971). *Statistical principles in experimental design.* New York: McGraw-Hill.

Winter, D.G., & Stewart, A.J. (1978). Power motivation. In H. London & J.E. Exner, Jr. (Eds.), *Dimensions of personality* (pp. 391–448). New York: Wiley.

Wrong, D.H. (1968). Some problems in defining social power. *American Journal of Sociology, 73,* 673–681.

Yukl, G.A. (1981). *Leadership in organizations.* Englewood Cliffs, NJ: Prentice-Hall.

Yukl, G., & Falbe, C.M. (1990). Influence tactics and objectives in upward, downward and lateral influence attempts. *Journal of Applied Psychology, 75,* 132–140.

Zaleznik, A. (1970). Power and politics in organizational life. *Harvard Business Review, 70,* 47–60.

Zedeck, S. (1971). Problem with the use of 'moderator' variables. *Psychological Bulletin, 76,* 295–310.

Ziller, R.C. (1957). Four techniques of group decision making under uncertainty. *Journal of Applied Psychology, 41,* 384–388.

Index

About the Authors

Kanika T. Bhal is Assistant Professor at the Department of Management Studies, Indian Institute of Technology, New Delhi. A Ph.D. from the Indian institute of Technology, Kanpur, she has been Visiting Fellow at the Sloan School of Management, MIT, USA, and consultant to several public and private sector organizations including the Fifth Central Pay Commission, the DRDO, the PGR Group of companies and the First National Judicial Pay Commission. Dr Bhal has also been involved with international assignments on behalf of the University of Birmingham. Her current research interests include leadership, ethics, culture, and values. She has published articles on these topics in various national and international journals as well as a book entitled *Making Sense of Personal Values and Organisational Culture*.

Mahfooz A. Ansari is Professor at the School of Management, University Science Malaysia (USM). Prior to joining USM, he held faculty positions at the International Islamic University, Malaysia, the Indian Institute of Technology, Kanpur, the University of Magadh, and the A.N.S. Institute of Social Studies, Patna, besides being a Fulbright Scholar at the University of Kansas. Dr Ansari has over 25 years of active teaching and research experience in the field of industrial and organizational psychology (OB/HRM). Besides having published about 50 articles in various reputed journals, he has previously written *Managing People at Work: Leadership Styles and Influence Strategies, 1990.*